DRIVE IT!

The Complete Book of

HILLCLIMBING and SPRINTING

Printed and bound in England by the publishers

Published by
The Haynes Publishing Group
Sparkford Yeovil Somerset BA22 7JJ England

Hard cover edition — **a Foulis Motoring Book** — ISBN 0 85429 226 8

Editor Tim Parker
Production/Design Annette Cutler
Illustration Terry Davey

DRIVE IT!

The Complete Book of

HILLCLIMBING and SPRINTING

Robin Boucher

Haynes

Foreword by Roy Lane

The past few years have witnessed an increase in the number of books published about motor sport. There are annual grand prix guides and reviews, driver biographies and autobiographies, books on rallying and autocross and, of course, on racing cars themselves. So far there has been virtually no coverage of speed hillclimbing and sprinting. Because this book is a first it gives me even more pleasure to introduce Robin Boucher as the author of this excellent guide on our sport.

Robin is quite the best person to write such a book. Having known him for some years now, I can verify that he has uncovered the 'magic' of the sport and reviewed it graphically. As an experienced commentator and reporter, he has been involved actively in all aspects, from timing to marshalling, from starting to scrutineering and even in driving. As a complete novice driver he describes his split second by second feelings and antics in a McLaren M10B Chevrolet 5 litre in this book.

I have been asked many times why I compete in hillclimbing and sprinting. It is a result, more or less, of having competed in most types of motor racing and coming to the conclusion that racing from point A to point B 'against the clock' was what challenged me most. I felt more satisfied with my driving and more 'competitive'.

In 1967 I decided to build a special car for hillclimbing. This restricted the amount of circuit racing I could do, because of the special type of car. I am a believer in cubic inches and have long used an American V8 in a McRae chassis to challenge for the crown of the RAC Speed Hillclimb Championship. For me hillclimbing is the precision driving and the relaxed atmosphere of the 'circus'.

Drive It! The Complete Book of Hillclimbing and Sprinting by Robin Boucher tells you all there is to know about this, the best, of motor sports.

Roy Lane
RAC Hillclimb Champion
1975 and 1976

Author's Preface

"To my wife Rosie, who puts up with hell during the hillclimbing and sprinting season"

I have now been involved in the sport of hillclimbing and sprinting for ten years, and often have been asked why I have found this form of motor racing so captivating. This is a very difficult question to answer, and even after a decade, I am still not really sure that I can put my reasons into 'black and white'. Perhaps it all started many years ago, when I was at school, for it was at that time, that the Wiscombe Park hillclimb first came into being. The first announcement regarding what was to become one of the top courses in the country, stated that, at last, there would be motor racing in Devon. Along with many other people, I imagined a race circuit, and so visited Wiscombe expecting to see full blooded racing. This, of course, was not the case. A hillclimb is certainly a race, but against the clock. However, by the end of the day, I was hooked. Somehow, being able to watch each competitor individually as he completed his or her runs at speed, seemed far more satisfying than watching a whole gaggle of cars rounding a corner simultaneously. There was a chance to examine the cars properly, and view the drivers at close quarters, whilst they actually drove at very high speeds, comparing individual styles, whilst at the same time knowing immediately who was successful. The bug bit, and has remained strong ever since, and as I have become more involved in the sport, I have come to appreciate the tremendous atmosphere that only a hillclimb or sprint can conjure. Where else can you be surrounded by some of the fastest racing cars in the world, driven by amateurs, who strive for perfection, yet retain above all the desire to enjoy themselves?

With sport of all types becoming increasingly professional, there has been a trend towards an almost bigotted outlook, which presumes that unless success is achieved, it has been a waste of time. In such circumstances there can be no friendly and relaxed atmosphere. Fortunately, this trend has not overtaken our sport, for although, in many cases, a season can be tremendously expensive, and involve a phenomenal amount of effort, a relaxed, friendly aura always abounds at each meeting. There are very few competitors who like losing, but whereas this is very obvious in many sports, it does not show in hillclimbing and sprinting. The sport is primarily for fun; if success comes, that adds to the pleasure. If it does not, then the majority of competitors will still have enjoyed their days' sport, and that surely should be the name of the game.

The hillclimb and sprint scene is always open to anyone, whether in the role of competitor, or just a helper. New faces have been astonished by their speedy acceptance into the ranks of the sport. It is a free and easy sport, but still grossly competitive. There is no love lost when a competitor is on the track, but always a genial atmosphere in the paddock; this, I think, is the reason why, every year, I come back for more. I, perhaps, have been luckier than some, for I have been able to follow the sport throughout the length and breadth of Great Britain. This alone has been an expensive exercise, but one I would not have undertaken had I not thought that it was totally worthwhile. I have made a considerable number of real friends, people I would probably not have met at all but for my involvement, and even if I were forced to abandon the sport tomorrow, I could look back on those past ten years and say that hillclimbing and sprinting sum up the meaning of the word sport, closely fought competition, in a genial and relaxed atmosphere. When the opportunity arises, please join us for a meeting. I think you too, will feel the magnetism and be drawn into the sport which has a special magic all of its own.

Contents

Acknowledgement

Many times I have read that 'a book is the work of more than just the author'. Never before is it more true than with this one. Unfortunately I can only single out a few in the space allowed. The following have my most grateful thanks, Chris Cramer, Roy Lane and my boss, Geoff Inglis, for his support in allowing me to take time off work to attend meetings. Severn Smith Advertising of Kidderminster for their help with my photographic work. Mike Carroll, Peter Bow, Peter Ashley, Chris Cox, Dave Harris, Allan Humphries and Andrews of Bradford for the loan of their competition cars over the years.

The many clubs and officials without whose dedication, the sport would not flourish and the drivers for the countless hours of entertainment and fun which they provide during the course of a season. Thank you.

Robin Boucher

1 Introduction

Ever since the inception of the motor car, it has been man's desire to drive faster and faster with his metal steed, and many forms of motor sport have been devised to enable him to do so. They range from out-and-out racing on both closed, and in the past, open circuits, to forest rallying; both in their own right, specialised and demanding sports. Although the sport of hillclimbing is amongst the oldest forms of competitive motor racing, it is still often misinterpreted by the general public, being confused with production trialling and sporting trials, where the object is to see how far you can coax your car up the side of a slippery, muddy hill. What, then, is a hillclimb?

Take a tarmac road, usually twelve feet in width, but sometimes narrower, wind it up as steep a hill as you can find, with a wide variety of twists and turns. Surround this road with natural obstacles, such as earth banks, stone walls and trees, and you have the basis of a hillclimb course. Next we must add the competitors, those protagonists for victory, in this, the most precise of all forms of motor sport. Their aim is a simple one; purely to ascend the course, from the start at the bottom of the hill, to the finish at the peak, in the shortest possible time. That the sport is precise is ably demonstrated by the fact that the competitor is timed to within one hundredth of a second, using some of the world's most sophisticated timing apparatus. It is a finely split time indeed, but as will be seen later in this book, a necessity.

So specialised has the sport of hillclimbing become over the years, that the modern car, for those elite few drivers, with the very special skill required to become a champion, is the type of machinery which would hold its own on any major motor racing circuit in the world. It ranges from 600 brake horse power American V8 engined, single seater, racing cars, through the less potent, but slightly nimbler Formula 2 based cars, right down to sports cars like MG Midgets, and a variety of saloon cars. The sight of a top driver fighting such powerful machines to the top of a speed hillclimb has to be seen to be believed. Adrenalin flows viciously, even amongst the spectators, as the frenzied projectiles twitch and flick their way, at alarming speed, past the most solid of objects. The driver will fight desperately to keep the car on the narrow confines of the road, in the frantic, and almost impossible task of achieving the ultimate, the perfect climb. This, then, forms the basis of the sport of hillclimbing, whose origins date back to just after the turn of the century, when a hardy bunch of enthusiasts, much to the annoyance of the local constabulary, stormed their then slow, but nevertheless exciting new machines up the public roads, completely ignoring their fellow motorists, who not infrequently were met travelling in the opposite direction. However, it was soon realised that a closed course was necessary. They quickly flourished, and from then on, hillclimbing took a large stride towards becoming the sport that it is today.

Despite the fact that most hillclimbs are narrow, with no room whatsoever for error, the speeds achieved by the faster racing cars are really quite incredible. Shelsley Walsh for instance, regularly records speeds in excess of 120 miles an hour, as the competitors flash over the finish line. In many respects a hillclimb can provide the challenge of a circuit race meeting, for the aims are the same, to complete a set distance in a time which is quicker than that of your opponents. There are, of course, many differences, the length of the course being the major one. Whereas even a minor circuit race will involve competing over fifteen miles, the longest British hillclimbs are of just under one mile, whilst some of the courses used in the past, have been as short as a quarter of a mile. Because a hillclimb encompasses such a relatively short course, the competition is intense; a driver cannot afford to make a mistake during a run, even a small one, and still hope to be amongst the winning drivers in the event. As a hillclimb is a battle between driver, car and the clock, each driver runs individually on the course. Although each driver runs alone, many hillclimbs are long enough to allow one, or even two more cars to start their climb whilst the original car is approaching the finish. This naturally speeds up the event, allowing the organisers to accept more entries, thus giving the spectators non-stop entertainment.

There are many hillclimb courses in Great Britain, each one varying in length, layout and construction, and each one presenting its own special problems to the car and driver. Each venue therefore is an individual one, largely accounted for by the terrain in which it is set. Without exception, each hillclimb course provides many different hazards that perhaps, apart from hillclimbers, only special stage rally drivers would meet in competition. The very nature of a hillclimb course suggests that it is surrounded by real obstacles such as trees, banks and even ditches, and often they are less than two feet from the edge of the road. Now imagine, if you will, a Grand Prix racing car, such as you might have seen competing in World Championship Grand Prix races. Very much at home on a race circuit, but not for hillclimbing, you might say, but you would be wrong. Amongst other exceptionally potent racing cars, Formula One Grand Prix cars are frequently used for hillclimbing. They make a daunting sight, as they rush between the natural obstacles on the narrow tarmac road at speeds of well over one hundred miles an hour. Almost frightening at times, their progress is meteoric. This is the real attraction of a hillclimb, 'ten tenths' motoring, on confined, and often bumpy courses, where the winners and the losers are often separated by a micro-second, and where the slightest mistake can mean not only defeat, but often a severely damaged car. However, despite the inherent dangers, it continues to attract a greater following year by year, with many competitors forsaking other speed sports to take up the challenge of a sport which happily has an excellent safety record. Naturally, with support growing, so too are the available competitions, with several National Championships and a host of non-championship events run each year. All the meetings provide a real spectacle for the thousands of spectators. Why do they support hillclimbing? Well, where else can you find a full day's entertainment, with the best racing cars in the country, often for less than the price of a packet of cigarettes? Yes, it really is a sport for EVERYONE.

Hillclimbing offers plenty of opportunity to take things easy as Lou Jones, wife of Surtees driver Richard, proves

One of the most successful cars of the 1970s in British hillclimbing was the Brabham BT36X powered by the Australian Repco engine. This beautifully engineered car, seen here leaving the start line at Doune, took its driver, ex circuit racing driver Mike MacDowel to two consecutive victories in the RAC Hillclimb Championship

One of the stalwarts of British sprinting, former champion Johnty Williamson is still a force to be reckoned with along with the Unirents Surtees TS11 Chevrolet

Roy Lane on his way towards his first RAC Hillclimb Championship with the Fenny Marine GM1

Sprinting

Hillclimbing and sprinting have much in common, in fact they could almost be called the same sport. Many competitors will split their season, competing in both hillclimbs and sprints, for generally a hillclimb car, will, with just minor changes, be extremely suited to sprinting, and vice versa. The sprint course itself, in many respects, is very similar to the hillclimb venue, although it usually features a wider road and generally is flat. This makes an airfield ideally suited for conversion to a sprint course, and, in fact, many of the regular sprint courses are located at both redundant, and operational sites. The added width of a sprint course makes for far higher terminal speeds; some of the courses which form a circuit, can be lapped at average speeds in excess of one hundred miles an hour. However, not all the courses are as fast, for with a large variety of cars to cater for, many venues will feature artificial bends to allow the less powerful cars to begin to challenge the might of the faster racing cars.

Perhaps the one disadvantage that sprint courses have, is that some are located at operational military bases, and unfortunately this often means that members of the general public are not allowed access to spectate. However, fortunately there are many venues in Great Britain, like the majority of hillclimbs, that are fully equipped to cater for the spectating public. Spectator support is growing year by year, which is not surprising when you consider that at many sprint events the fastest cars can top 150 miles an hour during their competitive runs. Often the racing cars howl by at these impressive speeds, within yards of the spectators, who are almost without exception, afforded a fine view of the competition. The format of a sprint competition is virtually the same as a hillclimb, although with some of the sprint courses being up to two miles long, there can often be four, and sometimes as many as six cars on the course at once, and occasionally the event is enlivened by circuit race tactics such as overtaking.

It is the sight of some of the worlds' most powerful motor cars in full cry, with the driver fighting every inch of the way as he battles against his relentless enemy, the clock, that excites both competitor and spectator alike. No better words can describe the sight of one of these machines being driven to the limit through the twists and turns of one of the many courses in this country, be it a hillclimb or a sprint, than these — it has a certain animal attraction. Many come to accept the challenge with their own car, be it a Mini or a McLaren, or just to stand at the course side and join the driver as he flashes by, working away at the wheel as he desperately attempts to find those vital fractions of a second, which he knows are there, but which seem so difficult to find. Even after seventy years of hillclimbing and sprinting in this country, no driver has ever achieved the ultimate, the perfect run. It is a target which everyone in the sport strives for, many very nearly achieve it, many do not, but all enjoy their participation. It is the target of the perfect run which brings everyone back to sprinting and hillclimbing week after week, despite the fact that it is impossible to achieve, even with the utmost dedication and effort. Such is the enthusiasm of the countless competitors that few abandon the battle, whilst newcomers join the ranks week by week. They all have the same aim, to beat that invincible factor, time.

The sport of hillclimbing and sprinting, like circuit racing, caters for all types of motor cars, and thus for drivers of all types, who despite contrasting in their selection of competition vehicles, have the same aim, to drive that machine as rapidly as possible, in controlled conditions. Although the RAC Hillclimb Championship basically caters for the drivers of single seater racing cars, and as such, all the top competitors in the sport naturally field such a machine, there are thousands of drivers who want to compete in sports racing cars, sports cars and saloons, not forgetting the dedicated band of vintage and veteran enthusiasts. Obviously it would be unfair, and indeed stupid, to expect a vintage car driver, or a saloon car competitor, to compete directly against the modern racing car; simply it would be a no-contest. Any hillclimb or sprint meeting is, therefore, separated into classes, to cater for individual types of machines. Each class will carry its own awards for the fastest drivers within the category, thus ensuring, that whatever his or her choice of car, a competitor attends a meeting with at least a small possibility of success. Due to the fact that there are many venues in the country, administered by a wide variety of motor clubs, classes can, and often are, varied. If the meeting is a championship qualifying round, then the championship classes will be run, but at a non-championship round the organisers are free to choose their own class divisions, and often, in an effort to attract new blood to the sport, will include a class for standard road going cars, or rally cars, thus allowing everyday transport to compete in an event with a chance of success. Other clubs' might well place the emphasis on vintage and veteran cars, or even run a separate class for one particular marque, for example the class for Bugattis at Prescott. The several types of competitive motor car, ranging from single seater racing cars, through sports racing cars, to sports and saloon cars, will provide the basic classes for any event, although they are often sub-divided at various capacity levels, in an effort to make each class more competitive and exciting, to driver and spectator alike.

Saloon Car Classes

The saloon car classes are usually amongst the most popular divisions at a meeting and will feature machinery from standard road going Minis to special supercharged V8 engined Ford Capris. At many events there are now classes for unmodified road-going saloon cars which enables a competitor to enter his everyday road transport and still remain competitive. Amongst the modified saloons, the classes are often separated at the 1300cc size, with the smaller engined cars such as the Mini Cooper S and the Hillman Imp directly in contention with each other, whilst the more powerful machinery such as Ford Escorts, Vauxhall Firenzas and even Jaguars will be in a separate open division. Over the last two seasons a new class has been added for saloon cars, catering for rally prepared cars, and this enables the man who usually campaigns his car in either special stage or road rallying to meet the hillclimbers and sprinters on even terms. This class has not only proved popular with the drivers who can use their normal rally car with no modifications, but has also provided the spectator with the sight of full blooded power-slides as the rally drivers use their normal techniques in preference to the conventional sprint and hillclimb methods, which are a world apart from those of the rally drivers.

A young man in a hurry. Terry Tattam lifts a wheel as he throws his 1 litre Mini Cooper S through Sawbench Hairpin at Wiscombe Park on his way to another class win

The Vauxhall Firenza of former Jaguar saloon car driver, Wridgeway Horton, has proved extremely successful indeed in both sprinting and hillclimbing, having been used in Northern Ireland, in special saloon car races

Saloon cars come in all shapes and sizes, one of the more unusual hillclimb cars being the turbocharged Hillman Husky of Jack Peat featured here at the first hairpin on the seaside climb at Oddicombe

Modified Sports Car Classes

One of the most popular cars for speed events has always been the Austin-Healey Sprite and the MG Midget. These will be found every weekend in the up to 1300cc modified sports car classes in direct opposition to such machinery as the Hillman Imp powered Clan Crusader and Davrian. The modified sports car class for over 1300cc machines really does cater for the bulk of the road-going sports cars of today and certainly brings more than its fair share of exotic cars into competition with AC Cobras, Ferraris, Porsches and Morgans, all eligible for the class. This not only brings gasps of appreciation from the crowd but also provides some exceptionally rapid hillclimbing and sprinting in the process.

The tremendously powerful fuel injected Cobra which is shared by Malcolm Maycroft and Brian Wilson seldom concedes defeat when it appears in the large modified sports car class

Although originally produced as a road going sports car with a 1 litre BMC engine, the Turner when fitted with a more powerful power unit can be a very rapid little car. Despite the smoke screen which it is laying as it climbs Prescott the Ford powered version of Jim Gathercole has been extremely successful

The ten year old MGB of Terry Osborn, a regular sight in West Country sprints and hillclimbs

Sports Racing Car Classes

The sports racing car class is the first of our open cockpit divisions and because it provides a useful stepping stone from a saloon car to an open racing car, the classes are usually extremely well supported. The majority of the sports racing cars are purpose built for competition work although it is possible to use such machinery as Lotus 7s in this class. There are often several sports racing car classes with capacity divisions at 1300cc, 1600cc, as well as an unlimited category. Amongst the two smaller classes the most popular and competitive vehicle is the Mallock U2, a car originally built for Clubmans' Formula racing on the circuits of Great Britain. There are still some clubs which run a sports racing car class in hillclimbs and sprints for cars complying to the Clubmans'

One of the prettiest and most successful sports racing cars in latter day hillclimbing was the Brian Hart Ford BDA engined Martin BM8 of Richard Brown, who took the car to a splendid eighth place overall in the 1975 RAC Hillclimb Championship

Another excellently constructed car the Ogilvie 162, built by Bruce Ogilvie, could easily at first glance be mistaken for a Mallock U2 which it often proves capable of beating

One of the most popular versions of the Mallock U2 is the one fitted with the 1600cc Ford Lotus Twin Cam engine. This particular car, in the hands of building society manager Stephen Madge, proving extremely rapid and a prolific class winner

Formula and these cars must use a 1600cc push rod Ford engine. However, many competitors have replaced the push rod engine with the trusty Ford Twin Cam or even the more powerful Ford BDA engine and the sports racing cars, thus equipped, are indeed faster than many of the smaller engined single seater racing cars. Amongst the up to 1300cc cars you will find several home constructed machines which are surprisingly rapid and give their owners a tremendous amount of fun, but these tend to be overshadowed by the Mallock U2s in the up to 1600cc class. The top of the sports racing car classes really does bring some fearsome machinery to the start line for although a few people still rely on the Mallock U2, it is usually the more sophisticated machinery which takes the honours. The pacemakers in the class are usually the purpose built sports racing cars, often initially built for International circuit racing. These are cars such as the Chevron, McLaren and Martin.

Single Seater Racing Cars

It must be the dream of the majority of sprinters and hillclimbers to drive, one day, a single seater racing car. The single seater division is certainly well supported with no less than four different classes. The smallest capacity class features racing cars up to 500cc; this may not sound like a fast or competitive class but, in fact, it is. The majority of the competitors in this class are using Cooper Nortons, produced for circuit racing just after the second war, and despite their advancing age, these machines are faster now than they have ever been, and provide great spectator value as they slide their way through the bends. In the past few years new cars have appeared to challenge the might of these historic cars, and not surprisingly, with advanced technology, have proved faster. Therefore, the up to 500cc class is usually subdivided into divisions for modern and historic cars, the latter being built before 1961.

Typical of the motorcycle engined 500cc racing cars of the immediate post war years, is the Staride of Dave Bishop, a regular competitor in hillclimbs

One of the prettiest cars in the up to 1100cc class is the Ginetta G17 powered by a Hillman Imp engine. The car featured here is amongst one of the most successful small engined single seaters in the hands of Sandy Hutcheon, here at Wiscombe Park

Believe it or not Rob Turnbull managed this demon manoeuver with his Brabham BT35 BDA on his first ever climb of Le Val des Terres. Here is real confidence

One of the most immaculate cars to appear in hillclimbs in the past few years was the Formula One Brabham BT33 DFV of Kidderminster garage proprietor Tony Griffiths, who later sold the car to Simon Riley for sprinting

The next step up the ladder towards the largest racing car class is the up-to-1100cc division. This is, despite the comparatively small engine size, a very rapid way to hillclimb and sprint, and it is in this class where ingenious home constructed cars, as well as purpose built machines, often feature. Amongst the most popular ware in this class is the ex-F3 circuit racing single seater such as the Cooper and Lotus with the 1-litre Cosworth engine, but these engines can be a slight disadvantage as they only perform well at high revs, and it is not always possible to keep them at that point through tight hairpins. The Hillman Imp engined cars such as the Vixen and the Ginetta G17 can be competitive along with the ever increasing number of supercharged Ford engined cars. Altogether, the 1100cc class provides great entertainment for both drivers and spectators and is certainly a fine training ground for the would-be National champion of tomorrow.

The penultimate single seater racing car class features the up to 1600cc racing car. It is here that we find cars and drivers well capable of posting some of the quickest times at a meeting and scoring points in the main National championships. The engines of these cars can be extremely powerful despite their size, often developing nearly 240 brake horse power, or the equivalent power of seven road going Minis, in a car weighing even less than one Mini! This class features a wide variety of cars ranging from Formula 2 circuit racing Brabhams to F3 Ensigns but almost without exception the engine is a Ford derivative, either the highly successful ex F2 Cosworth FVA engine or the Holbay modified Formula 3 engine. The chassis used are generally based on the circuit cars although like most of the single seaters, the suspension is redesigned to cope with the completely different challenge of hillclimbing and sprinting, along with such components as gear ratios. On a twisty venue it is not unknown for the up-to-1600cc racing car to set the fastest time of the day as they are certainly amongst the nimblest cars through the bends, but generally on a 'power' course they just lose out to the larger engined and more powerful cars.

It is in the large racing car class where ingenuity and painstaking preparation work are really noticeable. It is a class which leaves one wondering which is the best type of car for the job. Certainly there is the philosophy that the more power you have, the more chance you have of winning. However, many of the large Chevrolet V8 engined single seater racing cars are developing over 550 brake horse power; with this sort of power, control becomes a problem, particularly on a twelve foot wide road with no room for error. As in the previous classes, the choice of chassis is almost unlimited although there are very few people who use a large engine who do not put their trust in a modified Chevrolet V8 engine. The next alternative for this class is an ex Formula One Grand Prix car with the Cosworth DFV engine, but generally this engine, with a few exceptions, has not proved quite the answer to the Chevrolet or the smaller two litre engines such as the Ford BDG. Nevertheless, with the DFV engines, have come such delectable cars as the Brabham BT33 and BT37, virtually straight from the Grand Prix circuits. The last alternative for this highly competitive class is the two litre Ford based engine, such as the BDG or a Hart 420R and although these are less than half the capacity of the Chevrolet, they still produce over 270 brake horse power and by virtue of their lightness and much smaller size, can be fitted into a much smaller and nimbler car. Often they can more than make up through the bends, the slight amount of time they lose to the larger engined and more powerful cars, on the straights. This all adds up to a tremendously exciting class where the search for perfection is a never ending one.

Throughout any season new cars and engines will appear, often, as in the case of the five litre Repco engine, to challenge the supremacy of such established pacemakers as the Chevrolet and the Ford based engines. Certainly this class, like the others in their own way, produces tense and exciting hillclimbing and sprinting with often a handful of cars being separated by mere hundredths of a second at the end of the day.

Although the classes listed are generally the ones to which a meeting will be run, there are many organising clubs who may modify them or even add further classes depending on the type of competitor they are catering for. If the meeting is a round of the RAC National Hill climb championship, these classes would apply, but for example, two rounds of this particular championship are staged at Prescott near Cheltenham, the home of the Bugatti Owners Club, and at any particular meeting there you would also find additional classes for the Bugattis and Ferraris of the members of the organising club. Often these classes are run on a handicap basis, whilst at many meetings you will find both scratch and handicap classes for vintage and veteran machinery in addition to the normal divisions, whilst should the meeting be a round of the BARC Hillclimb championship, you would find many of the regular classes split even further to comply with the rules of this particular championship. So, as you can see, each meeting is slightly different regarding the classes, with each organising club promoting the classes that best suits its prospective competitors and its own club members. Nevertheless, there is always a fine representative selection of competing cars ranging from road-going saloons to outright racing cars providing a highly entertaining day's sport for all concerned, be they competitors or spectators.

2 How it all began

To trace the beginnings of hillclimbing and sprinting, we have to look back to the turn of the century, a time when the motor car was just starting to make its impression on the general public, although a vast majority still feared the fire breathing and noisy machines. That they would never surmount the capability of the horse for power and efficiency, was the general consensus of opinion. Despite this disapproval from the majority of the general public, it was not long before the motor car was to become an accepted every-day occurrence on the then, mainly dirt roads of the country. With the coming of the motor car as a social force to be reckoned with, came an equally burning desire for man to drive faster and faster, and to pit his skill against this new and rather unpredictable monster. It was not long before the Sunday afternoon sport for the honoured-few automobile owners consisted of private racing on public roads, a highly dangerous occupation, despite the relatively few motor cars in existence at the time. These unofficial races quickly fired the imagination of many a motor car owner, and it was not long before groups of intrepid motorists collected, to either race their fellow drivers, or to see who could travel a given section of road in the shortest time. Already the sprint was developing. These drivers quickly formed into motor clubs, and some organised events were held, the first and one of the most popular being at the Sunrising Hill, a public road in Warwickshire. However, there was one slight problem; the use of public roads for motor sport, even at that time, was prohibited, and although events still took place, the officials were forced to post lookouts, as the local constabulary, inevitably, would arrive during the competition. It was soon realised, that for hillclimbing to survive, a privately owned, closed course was necessary, and August 12 1905 saw the first of these come into being. The venue was Shelsley Walsh, now a legend amongst hillclimbers, and happily still surviving to this day as Britains' oldest existing motor sport venue still in active use. It was the Midland Automobile Club which inaugurated the Shelsley event in 1905, four years after their formation. The same club were also responsible for some of the events at Sunrising Hill, and as early as 1901, had organised an event at Gorcott, on the Birmingham to Alcester Road. Although, not realised at the time, Shelsley Walsh was to become the backbone of British hillclimbing, for from its first humble beginnings as a dirt road, the hill became tarmaced and then went from strength to strength. With an almost total lack of organised motor racing in Britain, Shelsley attracted fine entries and very quickly grew. Perhaps the greatest decade in the long history of Shelsley came in the ten years before the Second World War. Although, by now, there were other events for organised motor sport, both in terms of circuits such as Brooklands and Donington, and various hillclimb and sprint courses which never really proved to be more than temporary venues, Shelsley continued to grow. The Shelsley events became a major part of the British motor racing scene, and attracted not only the greatest drivers of the era from the home country, but also many of the top continental competitors. The crowds flocked to Shelsley in their thousands to see such revered names as Raymond Mays and Basil Davenport challenging Hans Stuck and his compatriots from the Continent. Great days indeed.

Whilst Shelsley and the hillclimb scene almost erupted with success, the sprint world was also growing, although no long term permanent venues could be found. This, however, did not perturb the enthusiasts, and

Memories of days gone by. The big Bentley is one of the real hillclimb cars of the 1930s, and is still in active competition today

One of the classic hillclimb cars of both post and pre-war, the Bugatti Type 35 seen during a cavalcade at Shelsley Walsh

A sight to gladden the heart of any enthusiast. Cornishman Ashley Cleave makes a farewell run with his wife in the 1937 Morris which he campaigned on the hills for so many years. The combination became an integral part of the sport, and is now sadly missed

meetings were staged throughout the country. The whole world of racing against the clock was becoming a most popular sport with competitors and spectators alike.

However, with the onset of the Second World War all active motor sport in Great Britain came to a halt, and not surprisingly in the six year interlude, many of the courses became overgrown and were in need of substantial repairs before being brought back into use. Even if the courses were a little the worse for wear, the enthusiasm amongst the competitors and officials was not, and it was all hands to the pump. The majority of the pacemakers re-appeared, having survived the last few stormy years, and before long, Shelsley was again operational, and hillclimbing was back with a bang. There were, however, many of the pre-war venues that were beyond reclaim for motor sporting use, and this meant a real shortage of courses. As the ravages of the war were mended, so too, the enthusiasm that had reigned before the conflict came through with even more force. The search was on for bigger and better machines, with which to climb Shelsley and the hills which rapidly appeared. With the advent of increased competition so came a dramatic development. 1947 was the year that saw the first RAC National Hillclimb Championship, a series to find the best hillclimber in the country, with events at a variety of courses, some like Shelsley and Prescott, superb venues, others not so good, but acceptable in a country still starved of permanent courses. The sprint world also developed with more and more venues becoming available, yet it is remarkable that it took a further twenty-three years before the competitors in that branch of the sport were given their own National Championship.

Nothing could now stop the sport from escalating and developing. The pre-war ware had been single seater racing cars like the ERA, and although they survived until the 1950s, their days were numbered, with the advent onto the scene of the little motorcycle engined Coopers. The 1100cc version in particular, proved the car to beat for many seasons, but then gave way to the American V8 powered cars. The progress was fast and exciting, times tumbled, interest grew, and still more venues were located and brought into use. The spectating public, although perhaps not quite showing the incredible pre-war enthusiasm, also started to return to view both hillclimbs and sprints. However the story was now a little different, for with the advent of new hillclimb and sprint courses, the choice for the spectators was greater, and with several motor racing circuits also staging meetings, the massive crowds witnessed at Shelsley in past years could not be repeated. However, as technology rapidly progressed, hillclimb and sprint cars became exciting machines to watch, and in latter years the crowds have begun to return, marvelling at the development, which is possibly faster than in any other branch of motor sport.

We have certainly come a long way since the dark ages of motoring at the turn of the century, when every motorist was a pioneer, and like the Western frontiersman, often scorned. We have a great deal to thank the competitive motorist and the early motor club organisers for, because without their special kind of enthusiasm, sprinting and hillclimbing as we know it today would not exist. If that were the case many thousands of people would be looking for other forms of entertainment.

Who knows what the sport holds for us in the next fifty years? One thing is sure, the pioneers' efforts were not in vain, for man with his modern machine is still fired by the same desire which caused his predecessors to incur the wrath of police and public alike. It is likely, at the present rate, that both hillclimbing and sprinting will continue to expand for many years to come. Even with a large number of venues now available, and several meetings each weekend, there are still competitors who fail to obtain an entry and compete. This demonstrates the healthy position in which the sport finds itself. One wonders if the early pioneers could have forseen that seventy years after their rather shady encounters with the law, the sport which they thought was fun in the early days of the motor car, would become an organised way of life for thousands of people in the 1970s. I rather doubt it, but we do owe them a lot.

3 How to start

I am often asked, "how does one start in hillclimbing and sprinting?" This can be a particularly difficult question to answer at times. Obviously the answer is to start at the bottom of the ladder, not rush out and buy the first powerful racing car that you can afford; where is the bottom of the ladder? Before contemplating entering a hillclimb or a sprint, it is best to find out exactly what the sport is all about and the easiest way to do this is to join a local motor club which promotes this type of event. Once in the club you will find its members extremely helpful; they will be able to help you decide just which rung of the ladder you wish to begin on. However, having joined the club it would be a wise first move to assist the organisers of the events to promote one of their meetings, for that way you can get an insight into the total dimension of the sport. Any promoting club will welcome, with open arms, the offer of assistance, particularly as a marshal. It is surprising what can be learnt by watching the competitors at close quarters during an event.

Once the bug has bitten, you will probably find it hard to resist a chance of entering yourself but before you go too far and spend money unnecessarily, why not enter your own road car for a couple of events? If you are lucky, the club organising the event may be running a class for road going cars, if not, do not become despondent, for although your own road car may be totally outclassed against the racing machinery at the meeting, it will give you an insight into the sport. Above all else you will know if you enjoy sprinting and hillclimbing, particularly if you begin your career at one of the smaller club events in preference to a National championship qualifier. Do not worry if your times do not appear to be as good as you hoped for, nearly everyone is slightly disillusioned by their first venture into speed events. You will find that the times improve with experience; nevertheless, if you have enjoyed the event then you are well on your way to joining the thousands of hillclimbers and sprinters who compete weekly.

Once you have acquired a taste for the sport with your road car you will undoubtedly want to progress further, but which way do you then go, particularly if you have limited resources? Many of the top hillclimbers and sprinters of today have started off in the saloon car class and the most popular choice of vehicles, here, is undoubtedly a Mini. If you have the knowledge and facilities to build your own car it can be an advantage, but do not worry if you have not, for at the end of a season you will see many competition cars advertised, often at reasonable sums and it is one of these which can give you an inexpensive start in the sport. Before you race your car, of course, you will, as mentioned, be joining a motor club. You will also need a Competitions Licence, which is available with no difficulty from the Motor Sport Division of the RAC, the governing body of British motor sport, and a crash helmet. Once again do not be disillusioned by your performance at your first few meetings, for the art of sprinting and hillclimbing is an extremely fine one and the polished precision shown by the pacemakers is usually the result of many years of practice. Once on your way the choice is then unlimited, for having graduated from your saloon you can possibly go directly into single seater racing cars, preferably an 1100cc car, or alternatively you might like to try a modified sports car or even a sports racing machine. Whichever way you go, remember the larger the engine the easier it is to get into trouble. The saying "Don't run before you can walk", is especially apt; the golden rule is one of progressing gently at your own pace. You will find some people can learn both a new car and a new course quicker than others; it may take you a little longer. It is inevitable that you will spin the car at some time or another, it happens to even the champions, but try to perfect a smooth driving style; do not throw the car sideways, it may be the quickest way around bends in special stage rallying or autocross, but it is always the tidiest driver who wins in hillclimbs and sprints, often the winner looking visibly slower than some other cars on the course. There is a saying that "the smoothest and quickest drivers always look slow." Above all, do not be afraid to ask your fellow competitors for help and guidance; you will find that almost without exception they are everyday, working people like yourself, who just enjoy driving as fast as they can in competition. Generally the whole sprint and hillclimb fraternity are at a meeting with one aim; to enjoy themselves and make new friends. Why not come and join us, you never know, in a few years time you might be the National sprint or hillclimb champion!

The rewards

When one looks at the cars which contest the National sprint and hillclimb championships it is obvious that these vehicles, being the cream of the sport, are rather expensive. In the majority of cases this is true; it is often thought that the rewards for success must be suitably commensurate with the cost of the competing cars. This is far from true, for hillclimbing and sprinting is still very much an amateur sport with no real professional involvement and at the majority of the meetings the prize money, even for the fastest man of the day, will fail to cover his costs for the day's sport. Why then do these competitors still compete? The answer is a simple one; enjoyment, satisfaction and that built-in desire to always improve on their best no matter what. It is true that the winners of each class usually receive a small trophy and occasionally a minimal amount of prize money, but both these incentives are secondary compared to the desire to enjoy themselves and drive faster than ever before.

There are, however, several goals which the sprinter and hillclimber can aim for, and of all the targets, one stands head and shoulders above the rest, the RAC National Hillclimb Championship victory, the supreme reward to any hillclimber. As its name suggests, the RAC Championship is the major series of the year and is contested by the fastest racing cars. Always it can be relied upon to produce a very close result at each of the fifteen qualifying rounds. This series, in itself, is a real challenge of man and his machine. To qualify to score points in the special championship run-off at the end of each meeting, a driver must be amongst the fastest ten cars of the day in his normal class runs, therefore, even the smallest mistake in the normal runs can rob a driver of his chance to score National championship points. Once in the top ten, his previous times for the day are discarded and each competitor takes two runs, the fastest to count, with the overall winner of the run-off scoring ten points; nine points to the second man and so forth to one point for the tenth finisher. Such is the pace of these run-offs that often less than two seconds covers the whole of the ten qualifiers, and it is not unknown for the outright course record to be broken during the championship run-off. The RAC Hillclimb Championship, being the national series, is contested throughout the British Isles with the championship chasers visiting Scotland, Ireland, Wales and the Channel Islands as well as a selection of venues in England, and there can be no doubt that it is a hard and challenging series. Whoever wins the championship, joins such all-time greats of British hillclimbing as Tony Marsh, David Good, David Hepworth, Sir Nicholas Williamson, Mike MacDowel and Roy Lane; all RAC hillclimb champions and each one of them winning the championship in their own inimitable style.

For the sprint exponent, the RAC also stage their own Sprint Championship over a variety of venues from the Midlands to the North and South of England, although unlike the Hillclimb Championship, there are no rounds outside England. The series is usually contested by pure sprint exponents although at times the hillclimb brigade, where time permits, will also contest the odd round, usually making the sprinters work for their money. Over the past few seasons, the sprint championship has waned slightly but fortunately a resurgence of interest in recent years has put the series well on the way back towards becoming one of the country's premier National championship events for racing and sports racing cars.

That seems fine! If you have a single seat racing or sports racing car there are at least two National championships to contest, but what of the man with a saloon car or a modified sports car? Can he stake his claim in the championships? Yes, he can, with again two National series to choose from. The first National championship is promoted by the RAC and is run in conjunction with the main hillclimb championship, being known as the Leaders Hillclimb Championship, and is aimed at giving the clubman a chance of competitively contesting a full-blooded championship. For the purpose of the championship, the entry list is sub-divided into eleven different classes ranging from saloon and modified sports cars to outright racing cars, with points being awarded to the top six finishers in each division; thus the saloon car driver is in direct opposition with other saloon cars only, whilst

Road cars can provide a tremendous amount of fun in hillclimbing despite often competing against the fully race prepared versions

RAC scrutineer Alan Kennedy can also be seen competing, as well as working, at meetings and his forceful driving of this Morgan 4/4 always results in a run which keeps the spectators on their toes

the racing cars stage their own separate battle for points. As this series runs in conjunction with the main hillclimb championship, it again takes competitors to the four corners of Great Britain but should a driver wish to contest a National championship without too much travelling to meetings, the Guyson/BARC series is a popular contest. Again the entry list is sub-divided into many classes but the points scoring system is rather different in that each class is allocated a bogey time based on the class record at the hill at the beginning of the year. To score points, a competitors' actual competition climb time is deducted from the bogey time and that is the number of points he or she has scored in the championship. A very simple system which again gives everyone a chance of doing well in the championship, providing that they are relatively competitive in their own particular class. In addition to the Guyson/BARC championship, and staged concurrently at the same meetings, is the FTD Awards Championship purely for the fastest eight cars at the meeting and this series is run on very similar lines to the main RAC hillclimb championship.

Unfortunately for the saloon and modified sports car drivers there are no national sprint championships to contest but all is not lost, for the motor clubs in Great Britain are divided into various associations, each one encompassing up to eighty individual clubs and covering a reasonably wide area, such as the North West of England, and the majority of these associations of motor clubs promote their own hillclimb and sprint championships within their own area, thus again enabling the clubman to battle for championship honours, and avoid travelling the length and breadth of the country.

It may be however that as a competitor you do not wish to tackle a championship, and there is no reason why you have to, for there are always a fine selection of non-championship events to contest, and there are many competitors who would rather miss a championship event to compete in a local club meeting at their own particular favourite venue. Although it is a great feeling to do well in a championship series it is not imperative to enter, and often competitors prefer to avoid them, but whether you contest them or not, a good run will still bring satisfaction and enjoyment and that is the name of this game.

To the victory, the spills, Roy Lane celebrates a victory at Shelsley whilst Chris Cramer, mechanic Jeremy, and Alister Douglas Osborn look on

Hot dogs are also popular with the competitors!

"If only" whilst watching the presentation of awards to the winning drivers, Tony Griffiths and Richard Jones contemplate the day's sport

4 Some of the courses

Throughout any season there will be new courses added to the growing list of those already in operation, and sadly, occasionally active courses may be lost for various reasons, but on the whole the current, operational courses in this country, and there are far too many to list them all individually, are alive and well. Let us take a run through the country and introduce you to some of the more popular sprint and hillclimb venues, each one of course, different from the other, and each one providing its own difficulties and attractions.

Hillclimbs

Baitings Dam

Although this hill, which is situated near Halifax, is not one of the longest venues in the country, it really does provide an excellent training ground for competitors, and indeed proves popular with both the experienced and novice driver. Its short distance always produces close and interesting hillclimbing.

Barbon Manor

For many seasons now, the fast and bumpy half mile course at Barbon Manor near Kirkby Lonsdale in Westmorland has played host to a round of the RAC National Hillclimb Championship, and a great battle has always ensued. The hill itself frequently sees speeds of over one hundred miles an hour achieved shortly before the driver slams on the brakes for a vicious hairpin bend, which leads to the finish straight. At the time of writing, the course record from a standing start stands at a fraction under eighty miles per hour average, and the sight of the top hillclimbers battling for championship points on this hill each May is not to be missed. In addition to the annual hillclimb championship round for cars, this hill is also used once a year for a motorcycle hillclimb, which features the fastest hillclimb and sprint machines in the country.

Bouley Bay

Possibly one of the country's most beautiful hillclimb venues, the Bouley Bay course lies at the North of the island of Jersey, and the thousand yards of public road, which twist and turn their way through the wooded cliff climb really do present a large problem for the visiting drivers from the mainland. In particular, those who attend just the one hillclimb championship round each season suffer from a lack of practice. The start itself is alongside the small and picturesque harbour, whilst, after a steep climb, the finish line overlooks the French coast; a breathtaking view. All-in-all Bouley Bay must rate as one of the most difficult hills in the championship, and with several club events also staged throughout the year, always on a Thursday incidently, the hill certainly provides a tremendous amount of entertainment for drivers and spectators alike, being especially popular with the hoards of visiting tourists.

BARBON MANOR

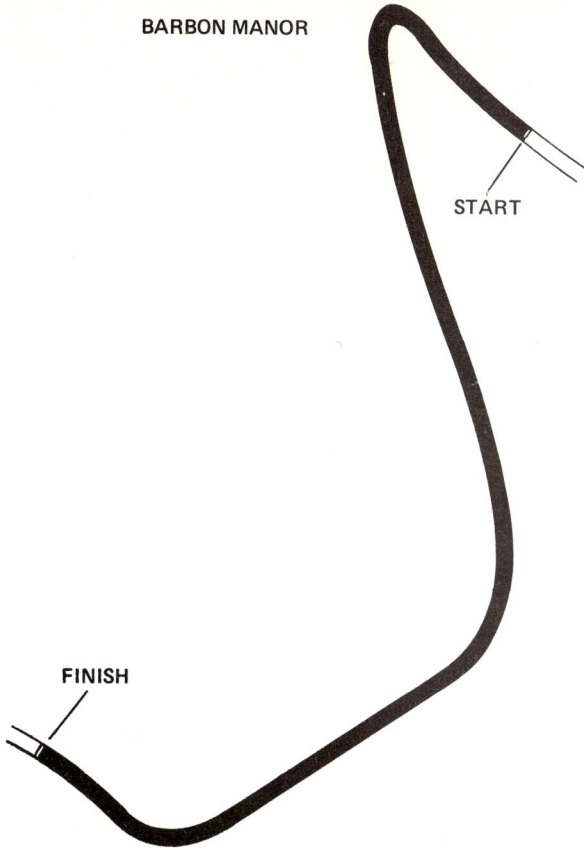

START

BARBON MANOR
Location: Barbon Manor Drive, 3 miles from Kirkby Lonsdale
Length of hill: 880 yards

FINISH

BOULEY BAY

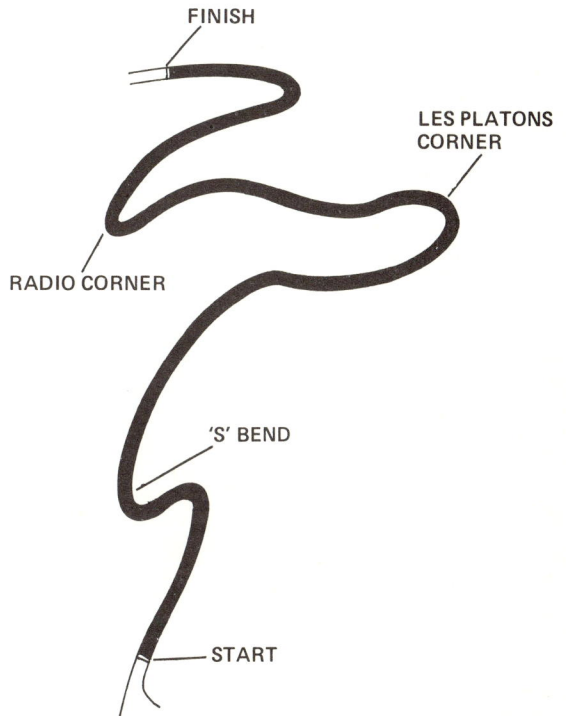

FINISH

LES PLATONS
CORNER

RADIO CORNER

'S' BEND

START

BOULEY BAY
Location: 1 mile from Trinity, North coast of Jersey
Length of hill: 1011 yards

Former sports racing car driver
Noel Le Tissier looking in
complete control of his McLaren
M10B at Bouley Bay

Cadwell Park

Basically Cadwell Park is one of the most difficult motor racing circuits in Great Britain, and like so many race tracks can also provide a sprint course, but Cadwell can even do better than this, for once a year the hilly part of the circuit is adapted to make one of the longest and fastest hillclimbs in the country, for although in parts the course is slow and extremely tricky, the climb to the finish line, on part of the actual racing circuit, is the fastest stretch on any British hillclimb with speeds in the region of one hundred and fifty miles an hour providing a tremendous spectacle. The Cadwell hillclimb, situated close to Lincoln, is a qualifying round for the Guyson/BARC Hillclimb Championship, with the event usually taking place on the August bank holiday Sunday, whilst in the past, the previous day has seen the sprint championship brigade present at the venue to do battle over the separate sprint course, which plays host to the RAC Sprint Championship.

Castle Howard

Castle Howard is yet another of the many hills in the North of England which have proved to be a good training ground for drivers wishing to compete at larger events. Again the venue is one of the shorter courses in length, but always attracts a fine entry for the meetings staged there. The hill itself is situated near Malton which makes it particularly convenient for the vast number of Northern drivers who support hillclimbing.

Craigantlet

The Craigantlet course, just eight miles from Belfast, is the only Irish hill to play host to the RAC Hillclimb Championship. It also provides the championship contenders with the longest venue in the series, being just under one mile in length. The course itself consists again of public roads, and is one of the faster climbs featuring a flat out crossing of a road junction which often sees the faster cars airborn, and certainly provides the spectator with an all-action meeting.

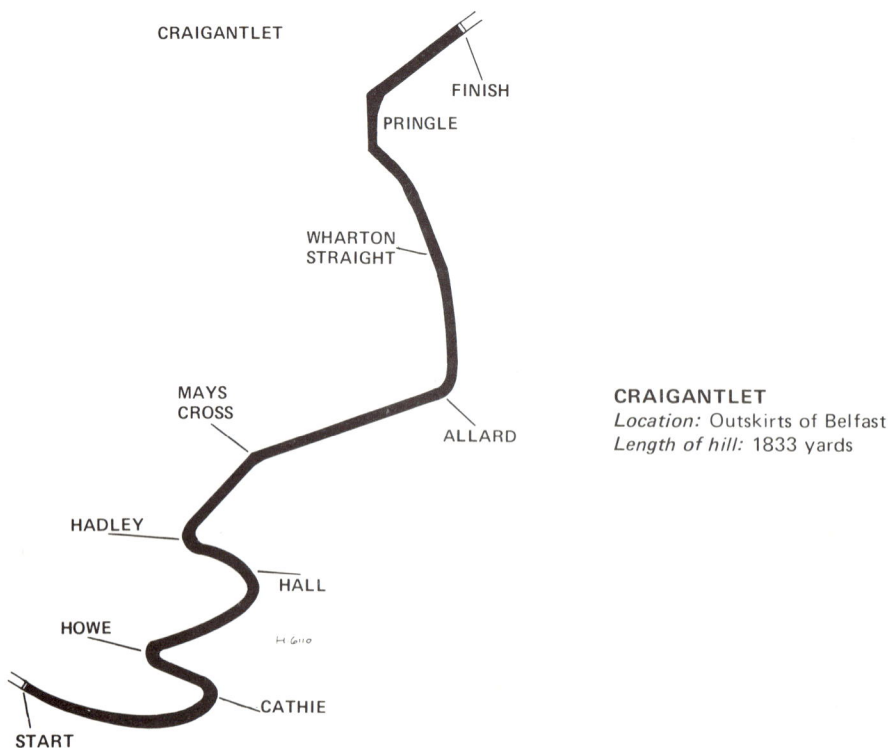

CRAIGANTLET

FINISH

PRINGLE

WHARTON
STRAIGHT

MAYS
CROSS

ALLARD

HADLEY

HALL

HOWE

H 6110

CATHIE

START

CRAIGANTLET
Location: Outskirts of Belfast
Length of hill: 1833 yards

Creg-Ny-Baa

The Isle of Man TT course for motorcycles is a magical name within the ranks of the two-wheeled enthusiast, and in the last few years the car exponents have been fortunate to be able to utilise a part of this course for one of the country's quickest hillclimbs. The venue, as one might expect from the reputation of the motorcycle course, is a very demanding one indeed, with some very rapid straights being punctuated by some equally vicious bends during the up to three and a half mile course. This venue always attracts a fine entry from the mainland, despite the fact that it is not a national championship qualifying event.

Doune

Just eight miles from Stirling in Scotland lies the magnificent Doune Park, containing a host of family entertainment, from a superbly laid-out garden centre, to a motor museum stocked with delectable machinery, and in addition, one of the country's most difficult and daunting hillclimbs. The Doune course is amongst the narrowest in the RAC Hillclimb Championship series, with little room for mistake in its three quarters of a mile ascent. This only tends to raise the agressiveness of the competitors, and to see a single seater racing car cresting the notorious rise at East Brae in full cry is one of the all time great sights of British hillclimbing. In addition to a magnificent course, fine viewing areas, with a chance to almost touch the cars as they hurtle by, one can savour the unique atmosphere of a Scottish meeting set in beautiful surroundings. A day at Doune is a day to remember.

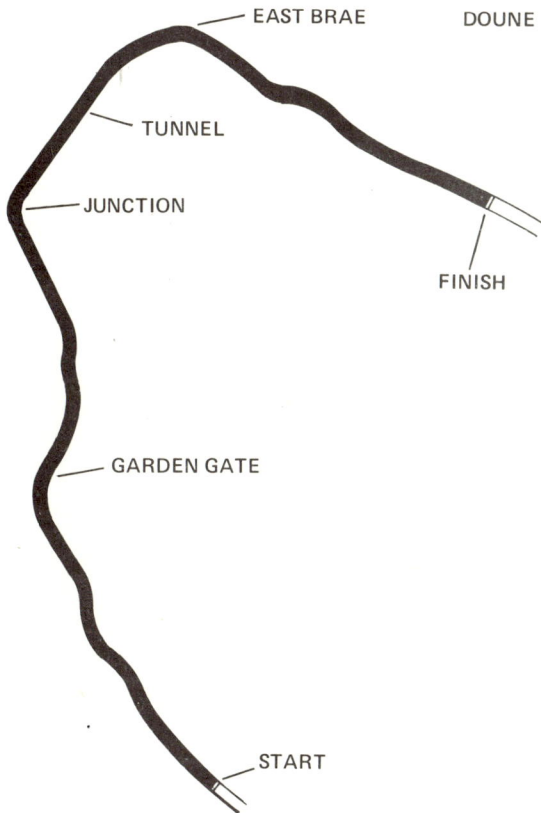

DOUNE
Location: 8 miles North West of Stirling
Length of hill: 1414 yards

Scottish hillclimb champion Alan Thomson, sweeps his Chevron B17 through the tricky Junction bend at Doune, a corner which has seen even the best drivers in the country in trouble at times

Fintray

That hillclimbing in Scotland is popular, cannot be denied, for to add to the excellent Doune meetings we also have the Fintray course, near Aberdeen, which although not used in the National championship, stages rounds of the local hillclimb championship series, always attracting the best of the Scottish drivers, with often the Sassenachs from South of the border also making the trip to challenge the local men on their home ground.

Great Auclum

At the time of writing a shadow lies over the unique quarter of a mile Great Auclum course near Reading, for it is possible that it may never be used again. This would be a great shame, for the bumpy little climb, which twisted its way like a slalom skier between ominously close trees, and contained a real wall of death banking, has been an integral part of the RAC Hillclimb Championship for many seasons. It was Great Auclum, which although only staged once a year, always produced a shock result; even the pundits would be amazed by the way that this oft criticised, but really loved hill, would upset the form book, and certainly should the course become inoperative, it will long be remembered by all those people who were ever lucky enough to spend a day there.

Gurston Down

The Gurston Down course at Broadchalk near Salisbury is amongst one of the youngest hills in existence, and came about through the determination of the landowners, the incredibly enthusiastic Hitchins brothers, and the South Western Centre of the BARC. The Gurston Down course is unique, for as its name suggests there is a downhill section, in fact just after the start line, and the faster racing cars sweep into the tricky bottom bend at some one hundred and twenty miles an hour, only then to be confronted by a vicious right-hand bend, and a steep climb. There is no doubt that the eleven hundred yard Gurston course is amongst one of the fastest in the country, and from the spectators area it is possible to see the vast majority of this exciting course.

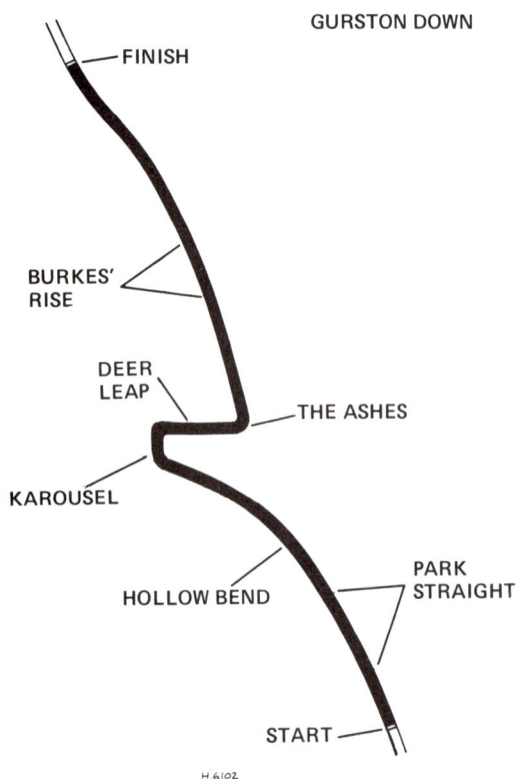

GURSTON DOWN

FINISH

BURKES'
RISE

DEER
LEAP
                    THE ASHES

KAROUSEL

                    PARK
                    STRAIGHT
HOLLOW BEND

START

H.6102

GURSTON DOWN
Location: Broadchalke, 9 miles South West of Salisbury
Length of hill: 1160 yards

The Alpina BMW powered Chevron B19 sports racing car used by former RAC Hillclimb Champion Mike MacDowel in 1975 takes a very close line at The Ashes during a climb of Gurston Down

Harewood

Harewood Hillclimb near Leeds is the competition home of the Yorkshire Centre of the BARC, and as one would expect from the club which has done so much to put British hillclimbing on the map, the course is second to none, with a fantastic view of virtually the whole of the climb for the spectators. The Harewood hill is unique, in that the paddock for the competitors is at the top of the course rather than at the bottom, by the start line, as is normal, but a link road to the start of the eleven hundred yard climb means an all action meeting. The course itself must be rated as one of the top six in British hillclimbing, and this is reflected in the standard of the entry for every meeting. The course plays host to the RAC Hillclimb Championship and during the year also stages rounds of the BARC Hillclimb Championship. The BARC Championship is administered by the home club, and fittingly the last meeting of the year at Harewood also provides the finale to the BARC series. In addition to a full day's hillclimbing, the organising club can always be guaranteed to provide further family entertainment, for scarcely a meeting goes by without a fairground, or a model aircraft display, or some such activity which adds up to a full day out for the whole family.

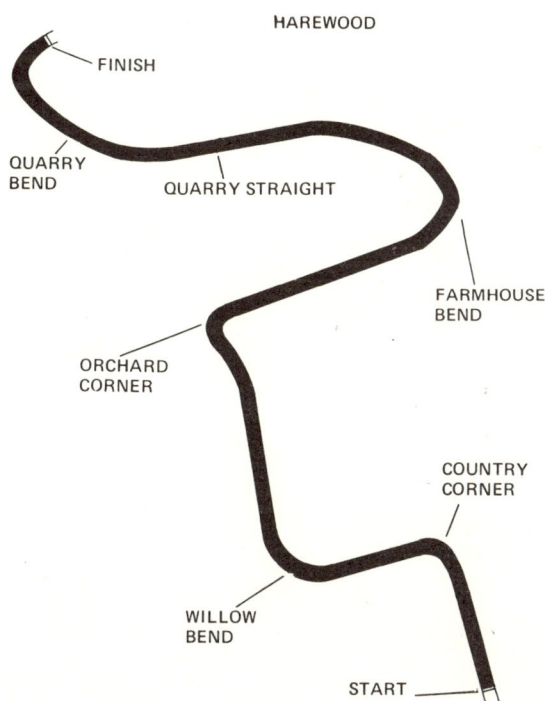

HAREWOOD
FINISH
QUARRY BEND
QUARRY STRAIGHT
FARMHOUSE BEND
ORCHARD CORNER
COUNTRY CORNER
WILLOW BEND
START

HAREWOOD
Location: Near Wetherby, Yorkshire
Length of hill: 1100 yards

Understeer can be a big problem to hillclimbers. Roy Lane, here, struggles to get the front end of his Fenny Marine GM1 pointing the right way as he takes the last bend at Harewood, Yorkshires' premier hillclimb

Hemerdon

The Hemerdon Hillclimb is again very much of a club event venue, being set in a mine not far from Plymouth. Due to the nature of the course the very potent racing cars are not permitted to compete there, but there is always a fine selection of saloon and sports cars to do battle at each event. The course is not one of the easiest in the country, despite its short length, but does make an ideal training ground for the novice driver.

Kinkell

The Kinkell venue is situated at a private caravan site at St. Andrews in Scotland, and again is a popular venue for Scottish competitors, despite not being on a par with Doune.

Les Val Des Terres

Les Val Des Terres is the second of the Channel Islands hills to stage a round of the RAC Hillclimb Championship, and like Jersey's Bouley Bay climb, the Guernsey venue utilises closed public roads. The start of the course, which is half a mile in length, and again wider than the majority of the mainland venues, is right on the harbour side at St. Peter Port, adjacent to the local brewery (handy!). The course twists its way through an almost unbelievable selection of bends, finishing high on the hill overlooking the harbour. This course is almost certainly the most difficult climb to learn, usually needing a tremendous amount of practice before approaching winning times, but this makes for some extremely exciting hillclimbing. Les Val Des Terres, like most of the major hillclimb and sprint venues, provides a running commentary on the event for the spectators, and this is the highlight of the always entertaining afternoon's sport, for it is this part of the event, more than anything else, that underlines the tremendous enthusiasm that the Channel Islanders have for hillclimbing and motor sport in general.

At his first ever appearance at Les Val des Terres, David Franklin took the first RAC Championship victory of his career with the Wendy Wools Huntsman March 742 BMW

Loton Park

Just eight miles to the West of Shrewesbury, lies the sleepy little village of Alberbury, which houses the wonderful deer park owned by Sir Michael Leighton. It is here that you will find the Loton Park Hillclimb, 1475 yards of twisting and turning tarmac road, involving a near airborn leap just after the start, and some particularly dramatic bends. The long sweeping climb to the infamous Fallow Bend is really the one to watch, as the faster racing cars twitch their way through at an alarming pace, within an ace of taking over control from the hard working driver. Loton must be regarded as one of the best spectator hills for action, although, unlike Harewood, it is not possible to see the vast majority of the climb from any one point. However, a walk through the deer park will reveal all, and there is a lot to this particular climb. It is here at Easter that the RAC Hillclimb Championship gets under way; what a hill to start a series with!

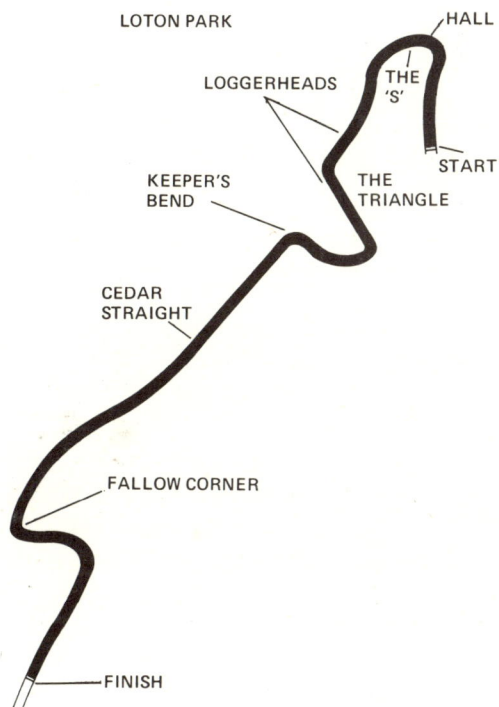

LOTON PARK — HALL
THE 'S'
LOGGERHEADS
KEEPER'S BEND — THE TRIANGLE
START
CEDAR STRAIGHT
FALLOW CORNER
FINISH

LOTON PARK
Location: Alberbury, 8 miles West of Shrewesbury
Length of hill: 1475 yards

The Waring and Gillow Chevron B32 Chevrolet of John Cussins approaching the very tricky Triangle corner at Loton Park

Oddicombe

In many respects, the Oddicombe climb is reminiscent of Bouley Bay, for the Torquay venue sees the start line alongside the beach. This must be one of the steepest venues in the country, for in its 650 yards, it climbs to the top of the cliffs, through three very tight hairpin bends. Unfortunately, due to the rather bumpy road surface, this is another venue which does not permit racing cars, but even the sight and sound of road going saloons will set the adrenalin running at Oddicombe, not to mention the faster racing saloons and sports cars, which really do take an incredible amount of controlling on this hair-raising hill.

Pontypool

At the time of writing, the Pontypool Hillclimb, which is set in the middle of the town's park and sports centre, is the only Welsh round in the RAC and BARC Hillclimb Championships. The course itself contains something of everything in its half mile run, a very fast straight through an avenue of trees, culminating in a tight hairpin around the famous stagnant pool. There are two other tight bends as well as a long sweeping left-hand curve towards the finish, which again makes this hill very difficult to learn. The building of the Pontypool sports centre has assured the hillclimbers of fine amenities, such as a restaurant, which makes the Pontypool course a pleasant one indeed.

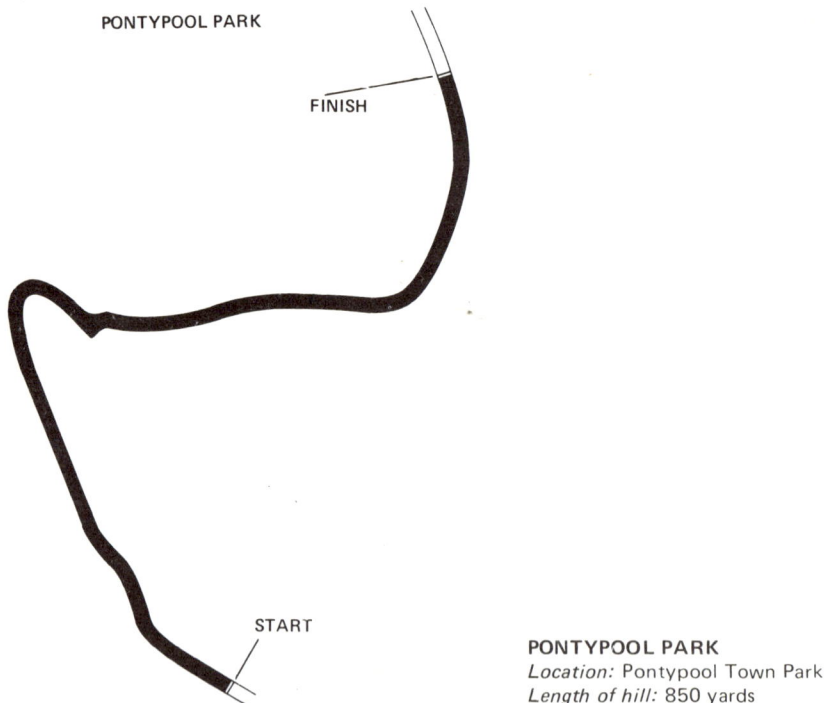

PONTYPOOL PARK

FINISH

START

PONTYPOOL PARK
Location: Pontypool Town Park
Length of hill: 850 yards

Prescott

Prescott, the racing home of the Bugatti and Ferrari Owners Clubs in Great Britain, must rate as one of the greatest hillclimb courses in existence. The venue, which is within easy reach of Cheltenham, is one of the classic hillclimbs in the country, having been nursed and developed by the organising club into, along with Shelsley Walsh, the home of British hillclimbing. It is the ultimate desire of any top class hillclimber, whether he be a saloon, sports car or single seater driver, to hold a record at Prescott, for the 1150 yard course has a special magic all of its own, from the on-the-limit Orchard Bend, where virtually all the faster cars drift alarmingly towards the barriers, to the tight and tricky Pardon Hairpin, where a slight mistake means a trip into the notorious sand. Rated by most of the championship drivers as one of the best three hills in Great Britain, the Prescott course is naturally amongst the busiest, staging two rounds of the RAC Hillclimb Championship, and a round of the BARC series, as well as club events and vintage and veteran meetings. The hill is set in the delightful Cotswold countryside, and can always be relied upon to produce, not only the best in hillclimbing, but also a delightful selection of Bugattis, Ferraris, and such highly desirable machinery. Certainly if you have never seen a hillclimb before, Prescott could well be the place to visit.

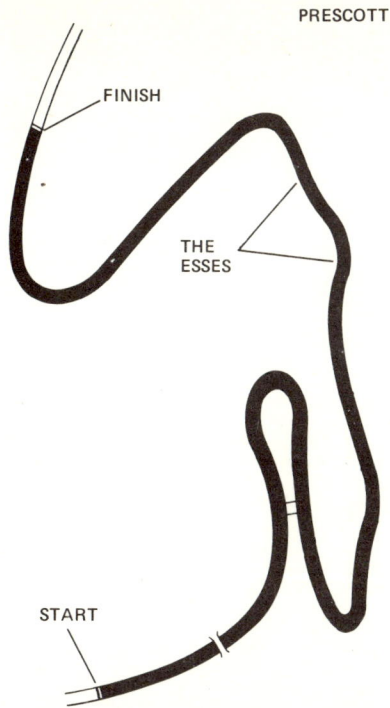

PRESCOTT

FINISH

THE
ESSES

START

PRESCOTT
Location: 5 miles North East of Cheltenham
Length of hill: 1127 yards

A traditional sight at Prescott,
the home of the Bugatti Owners
Club, one of the revered marque
in full cry on the approach to the
Esses

Ru.nster

Possibly holding the title of Britain's most northerly hillclimb, the Rumster course near Lybster in Caithness, is again one of the several popular Scottish hills. Being so far north, it fails, not unnaturally, to attract the southerners, but this does not prevent the Rumster hill from staging close and interesting meetings.

Scammonden

The short, but excellent Scammonden climb, is situated in the shadow of a dam, adjacent to the hustling M62, just five miles from Huddersfield. This course, like Harewood, features the paddock at the top of the hill, and like its Yorkshire counterpart allows a fine view of the competitive climb. The hill stages a qualifying round of the BARC Hillclimb Championship and club events. The sight and sound of the faster racing cars on this tricky little hill, really provides a stirring event.

Shelsley Walsh

Shelsley Walsh, near Worcester, is the magic name in British speed hillclimbing, for this one thousand yards of extremely rapid tarmac tells the story of the rise to popularity of the sport. From its humble beginnings as a dirt track, just after the turn of the century, Shelsley has progressed to become the king of British courses. The venue is one of the fastest hills in the country, with a top class driver completing his climb in just twenty seven seconds, from a standstill, having topped one hundred and twenty miles an hour in places. Shelsley is for the brave, for the high speeds, and the daunting high and extremely close earth banks, mean that there is no room for error, whatsoever; the slightest mistake can end in disaster. But the legend of Shelsley lives on, and will do for many years to come, for those of us who have witnessed Mike MacDowel in full cry with the Brabham Repco through the Crossing, seen Roy Lane's historic sub twenty eight second practice run, or Alister Douglas Osborn climbing in twenty seven seconds, will never forget it. Yes, Shelsley is special, and as Mike MacDowel once said, when he was the reigning hillclimb champion, "You may win everything, but the most satisfaction is gained by holding the outright course record at Shelsley." It may be the history associated with the venue, or perhaps the tremendously demanding nature of this high speed hill, which attracts hillclimbers and their supporters to Shelsley by the thousand; who knows? One thing is sure, Shelsley's magic is infectious, for once bitten by the Shelsley bug you will never miss another meeting.

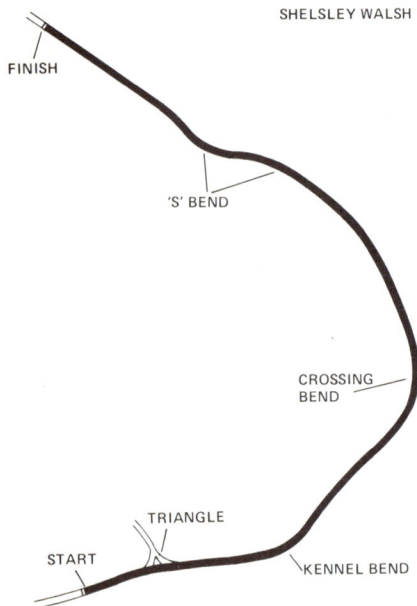

SHELSLEY WALSH

FINISH

'S' BEND

CROSSING BEND

TRIANGLE

START

KENNEL BEND

SHELSLEY WALSH
Location: 10 miles West of Worcester
Length of hill: 1000 yards

What goes up must come down. Having climbed Shelsley Walsh at a competitive speed, the competitors make their way down to the paddock en masse

Tregrehan

Situated on the outskirts of St. Austell in Cornwall, the six hundred yard Tregrehan climb, which has one of the best surfaces of any venue in Great Britain, never fails to attract the best of the West Country sprinters and hillclimbers. Being short, with one long sweeping bend and a tight hairpin, this hill is a great leveller, and often the fastest racing cars are challenged for the honour of setting the best time of the day, by the very rapid Mini Coopers, and a great battle nearly always ensues.

Trengwainton

If Rumster can claim to be the most northerly hillclimb, then in direct contrast, this concrete surfaced hill near Penzance, must be the most southerly. Just a quarter of a mile long, with two severe hairpins, the meetings at Trengwainton are always action packed, with the four wheeled competitors being joined by the best motorcycle hillclimbers, who in the past, have been known to show the cars a clean pair of heels in the battle for the fastest time of the day.

Valance School

The Valance School climb, which forms the drive to the educational establishment near Westerham in Kent, is unfortunately used but once a year, for it really is a fine little course, featuring some rapid straights, with the sting in the tail coming right at the end of the ascent, in the form of a vicious right-hand hairpin. Being situated in Kent, the meeting not only attracts many of the country's top hillclimbers, but usually the annual event will see rallycross stars such as Rod Chapman, pitting their skills against the established tarmac drivers, usually with more than a modicum of success.

Wiscombe Park

Not far from the Devonshire tourist area of Sidmouth, lies the beautiful Wiscombe Park estate, which includes one of the country's best hillclimbs, one thousand yards of tortuous climb, which contains no less than two full blooded hairpins, as well as a one hundred mile an hour straight. The real crowd pleaser at Wiscombe, however, is the notorious Bunny's Leap, where the faster cars momentarily become airborn just before a sharp bend through a tight gateway. This leads to much frantic motoring, as indeed does the rest of the Wiscombe course, which plays host to rounds of both the RAC and BARC Hillclimb Championships, as well as staging club meetings, to a very popular all motorcycle event at the end of the year, and to an RAC Rally stage in December.

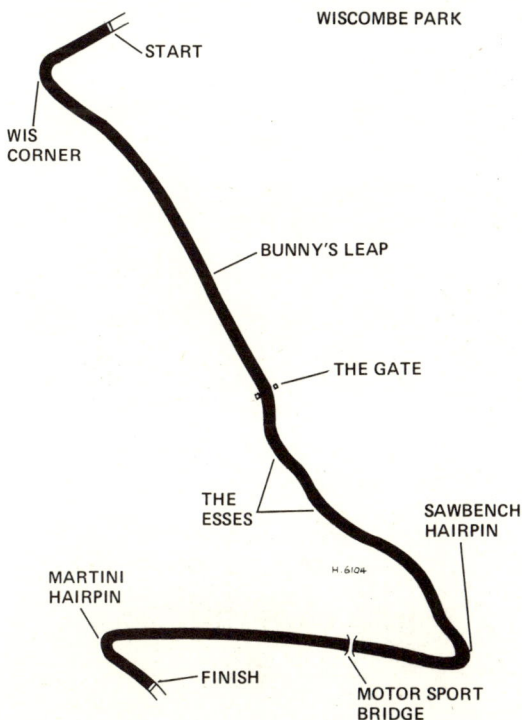

WISCOMBE PARK
Location: 2 miles North of A35 between Sidmouth and Colyton
Length of hill: 1000 yards

The sting in the tail at Wiscombe Park comes with the Martini Hairpin which Chris Cramer is entering with his 2 litre Grunhalle Lager March

Sprint Courses

Bassingbourn

Like so many of the sprint courses in Great Britain, Bassingbourn utilises the vast wastes of an airfield, which is converted into a race track for each meeting. The venue is situated not far from Royston in Hertfordshire, and forms part of the RAC National Sprint Championship series. Bassingbourn must surely be the fastest sprint course in the country, with the course record for the venue standing at an average speed of well over 100 miles per hour.

Possibly the most exciting of all sprint cars in 1976 was the Lotus 76 DFV Formula One car, as raced by the works, and taken into second place overall in the Haynes Publishing/RAC Sprint Championship by David Render, en route collecting a new course record at Bassingbourn

Blackbushe

This course again is situated on an airfield, and is used many times throughout the year for car sprinting, auto tests, slaloms and drag racing. Its location near Camberley in Surrey makes it an ideal venue for Londoners.

Brighton

Amongst the oldest sprint courses in Great Britain, the one kilometer straight sprint along the sea front at Brighton, has always proved a most popular event indeed. With two cars starting side by side, the once a year event can provide great drama and excitement, with speeds in excess of one hundred and fifty miles an hour often achieved by the faster racing cars. The spectator areas of this particular course are first class, with a view of most of the track available to the paying public.

Curborough

Situated near Lichfield in Staffordshire, the Curborough course must be the most used sprinting venue in Great Britain, staging a meeting virtually every weekend throughout the summer. These meetings include at least two rounds of the RAC Sprint Championship. The course itself, is an extremely difficult one with a hundred and twenty mile an hour straight, and a very tight chicane. Due to its popularity, the venue features all the public amenities, and a fine view of the whole of the course from the spectator areas.

Sprint champion Dave Harris applies a little opposite lock as he comes through the first sweeping bend at Curborough

Elvington

In the sprint world the name of Elvington in Yorkshire holds a special significance, for it is here that the annual World and National record attempts are held. The course for the attempts is situated on a wide open runway, and the length adjusted according to the record attempt, ranging from a quarter of a mile, to a kilometer and beyond. It was on this course that many existing world records were set, including three World records to the credit of Miss Patsy Burt with her McLaren racing car.

Princess Way

For some reason seaside courses have proved extremely popular venues, and Princess Way, Blackpool is no exception, with some very rapid motoring possible as the cars roar between stone walls, with little room for error. This venue stages a round of the National Sprint Championship and holds a special attraction for drivers and spectators alike.

St. Eval

Not far from Newquay in Cornwall lies the now disused airfield of St. Eval, which although rather bleak, makes a fine sprint venue. With typical Cornish enthusiasm, the local sprinters have over the years developed St. Eval, and now there are a choice of courses, the main circuit being extremely rapid indeed and providing a taste of flat out motoring for even the racing car drivers, whilst the bends have on more than one occasion been known to catch out even the most experienced of sprinters.

Talbenny

Laying claim to the honour of being Britain's most westerly mainland motor sporting venue, the little Talbenny sprint course, near Haverfordwest really is amongst the best venues in the country. Consisting of a narrow three quarter of a mile circuit, with even a hill to climb, the meeting always attracts the best in Welsh sprinting, although due to its remoteness, seldom sees the bulk of the English contingent. The course is a popular qualifying round for the Welsh Speed Championship, and an ideal training ground for drivers of all classes of vehicles, really demanding the utmost from man and machine.

Weston-Super-Mare

The sea front at Weston-Super-Mare comes alive once a year, to the sound of the fastest racing cars in the country, as the Marine Parade hosts a round of the RAC Sprint Championship, over a half kilometer course. Although the track is basically a straight line, the speeds attained over the finish are extremely high, with the faster of the racing cars often topping one hundred and fifty miles an hour, after just five hundred and fifty yards of motoring from a standstill. Again the spectators are well catered for, with adequate views over the majority of the course, of this not-to-be-missed annual event.

Woodvale

Not far from Stockport lies one of the north's most popular sprinting venues, Woodvale, again an airfield course which really makes the competitor work for his money. The venue stages several events throughout the year, and as one would expect from the north of England's most popular sprint course, also holds a round of the RAC Sprint Championship.

Wroughton

The Royal Naval Air Yard at Wroughton, near Swindon, provides a magnificent motor sporting arena, with the choice of at least two sprint courses, as well as a drag racing strip. Both the sprint courses are rated as amongst the best in the country by the competitors, and like so many venues, the Wroughton course permits some exceptionally high speeds. As well as a round of the Sprint Championship, the course is also used for club meetings and drag events throughout the year, but with the exception of the drag meetings, members of the general public are not generally admitted.

Pursuit sprinting can often provide incidents similar to those seen in circuit racing. Here a motley selection of cars look for the right line at Wroughton

Yeovilton

Used but once a year, the half mile triangular circuit on the outskirts of the Yeovilton Royal Naval Air base in Somerset, must rate as one of the best spectator venues in the country. With each run consisting of two laps, and the majority of the tricky little circuit visible from the spectator areas, this course provides a fine introduction to the sport of sprinting. In latter years the Yeovilton events have been qualifying rounds for the RAC Sprint Championship, attracting a superb entry of rapid single seater racing cars, as well as the usual excellent selection, like most sprint meetings, of saloons and sports cars. However, the Yeovilton meeting has one added attraction, for the event is always rounded off with the excellent knockout competition, which is a straight race between two cars, with the winner going into the next heat, this finale always proving a great crowd warmer.

Although the above list contains most of the currently used sprint and hillclimb venues, there are still many more throughout Great Britain that are used infrequently, as well as the majority of the country's major motor racing circuits, such as Brands Hatch, Silverstone and Ingliston, which stage sprints, usually towards the end of the racing season. With the sport of sprinting and hillclimbing growing in stature from year to year, the search is constantly on for new and improved venues. Throughout any season new courses will be explored, some will stay for many years to come, whilst others may only be used on a one-off basis. However, there can be no doubt that the majority of existing venues will be ever increasingly used in the future, as more and more people, each weekend, take on the challenge of their motor car, the course, and the ever ticking clock, in a battle to travel that lonely stretch of racing track, just a few hundredths of a second quicker than the next person.

5 A click of the clock

As we have already seen, the sport of hillclimbing and sprinting can attract the fastest and most competitive cars in the country, often battling over a course of just half a mile in length. With the competitiveness of the sport increasing as each year passes, the result at the end of the day, can only be measured in minuscule amounts. It is here that the RAC approved timekeeper and his crew, with their highly sophisticated equipment, come into their own. With modern techniques it is possible to time accurately a run over virtually any length of course, to within one hundredth of a second, and it is not unknown for this fraction of a second to separate the winner from the loser.

How can one achieve such remarkable accuracy? The answer is basically quite simple. On the start and finish line of the course the timekeepers will assemble an electric eye, similar to the photoelectric cells used in many commercial burglar alarm systems, and this casts a ray of light along the lines. The beams are then connected to a highly sophisticated electronic digital readout clock, capable of measuring time to an incredible one thousandth of a second or less in some cases. In this country, the regulations governing hillclimbing and sprinting permit a ten centimeter run-in before the electronic timing beam is broken, and so by the use of a specially constructed lining-up stick, or sometimes additional light rays, the car to be timed is placed in its exact starting position. It is now common practice for the competing cars to fit what is referred to as a 'Burt strut', basically a vertical opaque strip of metal at the forwardmost point of the car, named after Miss Patsy Burt, who initially developed the device. The aim of the strut is two fold, firstly to enable the car to be accurately positioned ten centimeters from the beam on the start line, and secondly to assure that the same part of the car which breaks the timing start beam also breaks the finish beam at the end of the course. With the digital clock reset to zero and the course clear, the competing car is given a green light by the timekeeper and course controller, which signifies to the driver that he may commence his run in his own time. Once the car is underway, the start beam is broken, which activates the timing clock, and similarly, as the car flashes over the finish line, the second beam is broken when the car passes through it, and the clock is stopped. This produces a time to within one thousand of a second. This time is rounded up to the nearest one hundredth of a second, except in the case of a car which is not fitted with the appropriate timing strut, for without the constant height beam-breaker it is not possible to guarantee the accuracy of the time quite so finely, as the start beam may have been broken by one part of the car, and the finish beam by another, so the time is rounded up to the next tenth of a second.

Such has been the progress of electronic timing, that at times no less than three cars at once may be taking their active competition run on a course, separated perhaps by just fifteen seconds. This presents no problem to the timekeepers, who in such a case would bring into use three separate digital readout clocks. Another innovation now possible, is the setting up of a speed trap at any particular part of the course, and this is achieved with a separate clock, and two beams spanning a distance of twenty nine feet, four inches. The time taken by the competitor to travel this distance is recorded on the clock, and by the use of a ready reckoner speed table, is almost instantaneously transposed into miles per hour, thus bringing into the sport an added interest. Often, although competitors are very closely matched in overall times, the speed trap can show that there may be a considerable difference between their respective speeds at a particular point. The search for improvements to the timing apparatus is never ending, for although the timekeepers are all amateurs, they, like the competitors, are always exploring new and improved methods of extending the system.

In 1977 the newest addition to the equipe should be in action on the hills and sprint courses, a speed trap, which instead of reading out in microseconds, thus requiring a manual conversion table, will in fact read out immediately in miles per hour. It is probable that even the drivers who compete every weekend, do not appreciate the tremendous amount of work put in by the timekeepers, for almost without exception they are the first arrivals at a meeting, and can often be seen laying the thousands of yards of cable that connect the timing apparatus, as early as six thirty in the morning, whilst at the end of the meeting there is a considerable amount of clearing up to be done. Even during the week the timekeepers are kept busy, for there is always routine maintenance to carry out, not only on the delicate clocks themselves, but also on the apparatus that forms the beams, whilst scarcely a week goes by which does not require one of the precision lining up sticks to be repaired. Add to this the fact that as many as a dozen car batteries, which operate the various electrical circuits, will be in need of recharging and testing, and thus you can see why timekeeping at hillclimbs and sprints is a very important job indeed.

The moment of truth. David Morris drops the clutch of his Ensign FVA and starts another run. The electronic photohead used for timing the runs can be seen plainly on the right hand side of the picture

A good start is essential, and although wheelspin with a large racing car is impossible to eradicate completely, it should be kept to a minimum, to provide maximum traction

6 The spectator

Although there are millions of people in Great Britain who have seen and enjoyed circuit racing, either in the flesh, or via television, the vast majority of these motoring enthusiasts have probably never contemplated visiting a hillclimb or a sprint. Yet these events can produce the drama and excitement, matched only by the top race meetings. Imagine for one moment a championship run off at a hillclimb, one thousand yards of narrow and twisty tarmac, where the slightest mistake usually means disaster, for lurking close to the edge of the course are such solid natural obstacles as trees and stone walls. Add to this the fastest ten racing cars at the meeting, who are just about to set off in search of vital championship points, with speeds often in excess of one hundred miles an hour in sight. This is the basis of a highly entertaining finish to a meeting. However, the championship run-off is always the grand finale to the meeting, so let us begin the story at the start of the day some five hours earlier.

As the competitors warm up their engines for the first of their two climbs of the day, the spectators will be flooding through the gates, to witness the never ending battle between man and his machine, and it is here that one immediately realises that hillclimbing and sprinting is for the family, for the admission charges, despite the fact that some of the country's most expensive cars are competing, are almost without exception, extremely reasonable, and often cheaper than a visit to the local cinema. Once admitted to the course it is always advisable to allow some time to walk along the spectator areas, and pick the best vantage point. The majority of hillclimb and sprint courses in the country allow a good view of the course, although some hillclimbs, being through wooded areas, do not permit views of all the track. However, nearly every course provides spectator areas at the most interesting parts, with the favourite spectator points being at the hairpin, or esses type of bend, where the drivers will be working overtime to keep their steeds pointing in the right direction. You will also find that most points will carry a public address system, coupled to a commentator, who will not only give the times of each competitor as he crosses the finish line, but will keep you right in the picture regarding the whole meeting, pointing out the cars and drivers of note, and describing the cars' progress in his view. At several hills you will find more than one commentator on the course, and no matter from where you view the contest, you will know exactly what is happening. Once installed at your chosen point, it is always a good idea to obtain a programme of the event, which lists all the competitors and their cars, the various classes which the meeting is staging, as well as the appropriate class record for the various divisions. With your viewing spot chosen, all that remains is to wait for the first climb of the day, and this will be heralded by the scream of an engine, and the protesting of tyres, as the first of the saloon cars fights its way up towards you. Even without the aid of the commentator you will be left with no doubt as to what is happening, and then suddenly the first competitor bursts into sight, the car sliding as he tries not to lose a precious fraction of a second, the tail of the car wavers towards the grass bank and the driver's wrists move like greased lightning to correct the slide. Already the front of the car dips under braking for the hairpin, and in what seems like no time at all the car is bursting its way on up towards the completion of the climb, with the spectators still a little breathless.

Already you can hear the next car on its way up towards you. The time for the first car is announced, and surprisingly it is not as close to the class record as you might have imagined, but the next car bursts into sight, and incredibly it looks far faster than the first one. Is it possible? Again the driver is fighting to prevent the car taking control as he powers into the hairpin, leaving the braking to the last possible split second. It must be quicker, and seconds later comes the time which proves that he was. Already you begin to see the fascinating attraction of hillclimbing and sprinting, and as the various classes progress, so the times become faster, as the saloons make way for the sports cars, and then the racing cars, and almost inevitably the first of the large engined single seater racing cars comes drifting its way towards you. With a wheel on the grass and the driver flailing the elbows as he applies first one lock, and then the other, will it spin? Sometimes the answer is yes, sometimes no, the margin between the two is a slender one indeed, but this time all is well and the car powers out of the hairpin with the massively powerful engine on full song, the wheels spinning as the power fights to bite the road. The car snakes alarmingly, but still goes like a jet propelled rocket. The rest of the class then follows, and it is here that one realises just what a close and competitive sport we are dealing with, as the commentators voice rises with excitement, the last car has taken the lead by one hundredth of a second. An incredibly small margin, but enough to lead at the end of the first runs.

However, all the competitors are allowed two runs, and it is only the best time to count, and so with everyone knowing how they stand at the end of the first climb, the second runs prove even more exciting. The leaders strive to improve their positions, whilst the rest of the class battle to close the gap. It is here that records are often broken, whilst spins and incidents can also abound, as a driver just steps over that minute dividing line between rapid cornering and a spin. This is all in the game, and certainly provides the thrills for the paying public. With the class runs completed, the championship run-off will be the grand finale to the day. If the meeting counts towards one of the various championships this must not be missed, as the fastest ten men of the day fight their way to the top of the hill, on two further runs, this time with championship points at stake. Often the ace drivers will save their best for these vital runs. Again the atmosphere is electric, as the slowest of the qualifiers leads away the run-off, and although he may be the slowest, his progress on the road is still almost unbelievable. By the time that the top men appear the tension is absolutely unbearable. Will the favourite make it or will he be beaten? Well again the answer is often supplied by the difference of just one hundredth of a second, but whoever wins, the feeling is the same amongst the spectators, the drivers and the mechanics. It is one of elation for the winner, and from everyone else the feeling that again man has triumphed over machines, and that once more the clock has been beaten.

At the end of the meeting as the spectators make their happy way homeward after a pleasant and exciting day's sport, the drivers meet in the paddock, exchange notes and unwind. This is often a good time to visit the paddock to view the machines, and the drivers. At many hills and sprints this is possible during the meeting, and certainly so at the end of the day. In addition to the competition many venues provide additional entertainment such as a fairground at Harewood, or a childrens' playground at Shelsley, and there are always adequate facilities for refreshments, and naturally conveniences for natural breaks! A hillclimb or a sprint must be an ideal day out for the family, at reasonable cost. Try an event, you will not be disappointed and will undoubtedly be back for more.

No matter how exciting the action at an event, there is always someone capable of snatchin' forty winks

7 A day in the life of a hillclimber

As the peace and quiet of the silent night is gradually broken by the shrill tones of the dawn chorus, the sun peeks its way over the horizon, and another day begins. Suddenly the gentle mornings' awakening is broken by the raucous scream from the bedside, which is inevitably followed by the appropriate mutterings, as a hand reaches from beneath the bed clothes, and takes an almighty swipe at the offending alarm clock. He misses, contacting the bedside table, causing yet further mutterings from our hillclimber for the day, who at five thirty in the morning, is wondering just why he is involved in a sport which requires such an early arising. However, once in motion, the human body is a wonderful thing, and it is not long before the wife and the children are also moving into action, and within minutes the kitchen is covered with a haze of steam, as the kettle merrily boils dry. At this time of the morning breakfast is best forgotten anyway, and with the taste buds revived by a quick cup of tea, the clock rapidly approaching six am, our intrepid family make for the door and the saloon car.

Opening the garage door, a trailer lurks in the corner, and neatly tied upon it is our competition car. Reversing the road car, the trailer is quickly hitched to the tow bar, and with much frantic action the wife and the kids are deposited into the tow car, accompanied by the usual last minute panics, "Have we got the passes?, where is the tool box?, yes, dear, I did switch off the water heater and put out the cat!" With all these last minute panics overcome, our racing equipe finally hits the road, and as we pull out of our Warwickshire home, we are faced with a two hundred mile run down the motorway to Devon, and our venue for the day. Fortunately at this time of the morning the motorway is relatively quiet, and we make good time, as the wife and the kids snatch forty winks, whilst the trailer gently waves in the breeze as we head south. We are due at the hillclimb at ten o'clock at the latest, and so really have to keep motoring and with the speedometer showing a little over the legal trailer speed of fifty miles an hour, we are making good time. At half past nine we reach the end of the motorway, and now all we have to circumnavigate is some of the best narrow lanes that the Devonshire countryside can provide. Eventually we make our way to the competitors entrance, and the long rough road that leads to the paddock. As we approach the entrance there is the usual mad panic, yet again, searching for the competitors passes, which will allow us entry to the hill, but somehow they always come to hand. We bounce our way down the mile long bouldered track to the paddock, the kids, who fortunately have slept for most of the journey, are jolted back to life, with the usual accompanying cries of "I'm hungry, Dad can we stop now." However, once on the final stretch to the paddock, there is no stopping, and as the rough road makes way for a cobbled area, which leads into the grassy hillside paddock, the rest of the family are deposited at a convenient building, whilst the tow car and trailer carry on into the parking area.

As always, the paddock is well organised, with each competitor, who has been informed during the week before of his competition number, being allocated his own parking space. Quickly this is occupied, whilst the early risers who have beaten us to the event, immediately crowd round with good natured cries of "Good afternoon," although it is still the right side of ten in the morning. The first job upon arriving at the venue is to make the trip to the office of the secretary of the meeting, to sign-on, using the sheet supplied by the RAC. The secretary of the meeting will also check to ensure that the competitor is a member of the appropriate motor club for the meeting, and will check the championship registration cards, should the competitor be contesting a particular series for which the meeting might qualify. Once the formalities are completed we are handed a programme of the event. This lists all the competitors, and often this is the first look we get at the opposition for the day. This is usually heralded by the cry "Oh hell he's here again," or similar words, all naturally in good fun. Upon return to the paddock it is time to unload the racing car, and with the help of the family, who have by this time hopefully returned, this is rapidly achieved. The car is then taken to the scrutineering bay, where the official RAC scrutineer will check the car over to make sure that it is safe to race. The RAC officials are extremely thorough, and it is not unusual for them to find a minor defect, no matter how good the previous week's preparation has been, and in this case there is a quick foray to the tool box, some hasty repairs are quickly carried out, without any grouses usually, as the safety check is for the good of everyone, especially the driver. Once through the rigours of scrutineering it is into line for the first of our two practice runs. Usually this is on a first come first served basis, and so we join the queue at the paddock exit, which leads to the start line.

At the same time the engine is warmed up, with a check on all the gauges to make sure that all is well with the car. The queue gradually becomes shorter, until suddenly, the paddock marshal is waving us down to the start line. En route, as we hit the tarmac, we stop and do a couple of practice starts, to just double check that all is well and to warm up the tyres which operate much better when warm rather than cold. The car in front of us gets off the line in a blast of sound, and a plume of blue smoke hangs over the area, as the tyres spin viciously in an effort to find some traction. As he disappears out of sight we gently make our way to the line, where the start line marshal will line us up with his stick to assure complete accuracy of timing. With the crash helmet adjusted, and the seat belts tight, we are ready for the off, and then comes the tensest part of the meeting, waiting for the traffic light at the side of the course to change to green, which signifies that we can start when ready.

After what seems an eternity, the light changes to green, careful now, slip the car into gear, build up the engine revs, not too much and drop the clutch, and away we go through the thousand yards of twisty climb. Just forty six seconds later our car bursts through the hairpin bend at the top of the hill and flashes over the finish line; not bad for a starter! As soon as the car crosses the line we switch off the engine and coast into the top holding paddock, where a hasty exit is made from the car as we dash across to the times board to see exactly what we have done. Yes it confirms our thoughts, a good first practice run. As there is no separate return road to the start, and competing cars return to the main paddock in bunches via the course, we have a few minutes to spare and it is always a good chance to watch some of the other competitors on the top reaches of the course, and a good vantage point is staked. From here it is often possible to learn a few things by watching other competitors as they tackle the final bend. Some look good whilst others certainly look ragged and wild. This results in a slower time, and whilst you feel that you might like to stay there all day, there is no time, for the top paddock is now full and it is time to coast down the hill and prepare for the second run. As you travel towards your parking space in the paddock you will be greeted inevitably by the wife and the kids, the latter delighted with his father's drive, whilst the former as always reckons you were a little slow off the start line, or through the first bend, and your practice time is still slower than the class record holder. However, there is a second practice run to come, and so once again the car is checked over and then placed in the line for the second climb.

The procedure is the same, except this time, as you drive into the top paddock, you are met by the family who have walked to the top of the course via the spectator areas, and so they are faced with a walk when you go back down the hill to the paddock. By then it is time to crack open the supplies, and take lunch. Although, as always, you have brought adequate supplies to sustain the troops, the attraction of the hot dog van is too much for the children to resist, and so you succumb to their frantic appeals, and in order to keep the peace, a trip to the offending wagon is made. Upon return, you manage to enjoy your lunch in relative peace, although you are constantly interrupted by your fellow competitors, who with their good natured ribaldry, can always be relied upon to throw even the most experienced and organised of families into immediate confusion.

In what appears all too short a time, the gentle music which has been playing over the public address system is interrupted by a call for the first of the competitors to make their way to the paddock exit, in numerical, and hence class order. As your class is one of the first at this meeting, it is back into action to warm up the car. The commentator gets into his stride, as he generates excitement amongst the spectators prior to the first competition runs. In what seems no time at all the hitherto comparatively peaceful paddock area is shattered by a cacophony of sound. It appears that every competition car is started at once, but with the waves of sound comes a certain feeling of excitement, and drama. Suddenly the stomach erupts with a butterfly like feeling, for in just a few moments comes the first of the runs that matter. As the tension takes over, all else seems to disappear from view, with even the children seeming to melt away, despite their obvious enthusiasm for the coming run. Into the car,

Martyn Griffiths and the family
indulging in a little private practice
at Loton Park

"Are you buying the coffee Bet?"
Roy Lane looks surprised as he
relaxes between runs at Doune

seat belts on, isolate yourself from the world, and prepare for the run. Again that line of cars seems to shorten, but it seems an eternity before it is your turn, whilst oblivious to your feelings the commentator is ecstatic, the record in your class has just been broken, someone has climbed the course faster than ever before, but somehow you do not want to know. The task in hand is big enough without added problems and worries.

Now its your turn, down to the line you go, not rushing things, gently into position on the line, the light goes green, and you are on your own. Everything seems to happen so quickly, and in no time you are stepping out of the car at the end of the climb, perhaps satisfied, or perhaps pondering about the slide at the esses. It is straight over to the board to look at the time and compare notes with the other drivers of your class who are already at the top paddock having made their run. At the same time you watch the rest of the cars in the batch. Soon it is into the car and back to the family for post mortem one, a discussion on the run, and the class position after it. Meanwhile as you unwind in the paddock after the first run, the rest of the meeting continues at unabated pace, and often if there are no problems with the car, the whole family can take a trip to a mid point on the course to watch the other classes before it is back to the paddock for your second and final run of the day. Again the tensions are the same, and it is a repeat of the first class run, hopefully, with a slight improvement, if not to the class position, at least to the time. Often with the fickle British summer, the weather can throw even the most organised of competitors into chaos, for if the course conditions should drastically change this can call for decisions galore. Can the dry weather tyres be left on the car, or is it now too wet for the treadless tyres to work properly? Should they be changed for the grooved wet weather version? This is just one of the many problems which may be faced during the day. Somehow all are overcome, and the event almost certainly, barring major disasters, is enjoyed by all the family, win or lose. Once the second class run is completed and you return to the paddock, providing there is no championship run off which you have qualified for, the next job on the agenda is the loading of the competition car onto the trailer. Again with the help of the family this is rapidly achieved, often before the end of the meeting, and so it is again possible to unwind by revisiting the course and watching the rest of the climbs. The commentator, still working busily, keeps you informed of just what is happening right the way through the programme, and for once, with the tension disappearing, you begin to enjoy watching your co-competitors at work.

At the conclusion of the meeting come the inevitable post mortems. All the drivers congregate to discuss the day's sport in genial fashion, but with a long trek home often to be faced, the children beginning to feel the effects of the early morning start, it is on the road as quickly as possible, often with the promise of meeting fellow competitors for a meal on the motorway. These social get togethers after an event usually typify the fun loving nature of all hillclimbers and sprinters. The friendly bric bats being thrown, whilst the talk quickly turns to the next meeting, just a week away. With everyone now feeling a little the worse for wear, it is back on the road and head for home. Fortunately with the motorway relatively free the homeward trip is not too fraught, and at last comes the familiar road sign which tells you that home is just around the corner. The wife is gently dozing, whilst the kids are flat out on the back seat reliving the day in their dreams. Reversing the car into the drive, the trailer is quickly uncoupled, and the racer locked away, as everyone dives indoors with but one aim, bed, after another enjoyable and satisfying day's sport.

So on the Monday morning, at breakfast, the previous day out is always the subject of conversation. Whilst the rest of the family look forward to the next weekend out, our intrepid driver has but one thought in his mind. How can he find a little more speed, how many nights this week will he have to spend on the car to prepare it for the next event, how does he beat the man who led him yesterday. All these thoughts go to show the tremendous enthusiasm shown by hillclimbers and sprinters, for they know as well as anyone that although they may achieve maximum enjoyment, they will never achieve the ultimate performance, and it is this which brings competitors and their families together week by week. It may sometimes look like a futile battle, but it really is fun as many thousands of people prove each year.

8 The organisation of a meeting

Although the stars of any hillclimb or sprint meeting are the drivers themselves, the unsung heroes of any successful event must be the organisers. It is their dedication to the sport which ensures the smooth running, achieved almost without exception, during the day's event. Whilst the competitor plays his part well during the meeting itself, the role of the organisers has begun as much as six months earlier, when the initial planning for the event was started. As in any business, there are many technical details to be planned well in advance of the meeting. The never ending pile of paperwork assures that the members of the organising committee are kept busy, from the first planning meeting, to the time that the results are posted to the competitors, often some seven days after the event.

As with any organisation, it is essential to achieve a happy balance on the organising committee, which will be set up by the club promoting the event. This is usually achieved with a fine selection of club members, often including former or active competitors whose knowledge of the sport is, of course, a great asset; as the comforts of the general public must also be taken into consideration. It is more than useful to obtain the assistance of some of the ladies of the organising club, whose views are greatly appreciated, and often they can make constructive suggestions that the men on the committee could well overlook. Although the planning for the event itself will start some six months before the scheduled competition day, the initial decision to hold the event will have been made sometime previous to that. With the ever increasing difficulty of obtaining a venue, it could well be, that the original decision to run the event was made a full year beforehand. Once the club has decided to run an event they must, of course, approach the landowner and negotiate, not only the date, which is mutually convenient, but also a fee for the use of the course. Once this is achieved the date is forwarded to an events meeting, where local clubs in the area organise their forthcoming events, thereby assuring that no two events in reasonable local proximity will clash. A clash could only result in poor spectator attendances, and loss of gate money; an all important factor in the running of an event in this age of ever escalating costs. Once the dates have been agreed they are forwarded to the Motor Sport Division of the RAC who will publish them in their annual *Motor Sport Year Book,* as long as they are arranged well in advance.

With the venue and the date settled, the next move is to set up a competitions committee within the organising club, to take over the running of the event. Such a committee will be chosen by the club members themselves, and will always include a representative cross section of members, all with a knowledge of certain parts of the problems involved in staging such an event. Often new blood will also be co-opted onto the panel, to learn the ropes, in preparation for events in the even more distant future. Possibly the most important of all the posts on the committee is that of chairman, for he has to control the often heated arguments which can develop at meetings, and ensure that no stone is left unturned in the quest for perfection on the all important day of the competition. Once the chairman of the committee is elected, the first important item on the agenda is the selection of the major officials of the meeting. The following posts are filled; the secretary of the meeting with an assistant, the clerk of the course with an assistant, chief course marshal and chief paddock marshals, both again with assistants, a press, publicity and public relations officer, a chief spectator marshal, at least two club stewards, a chief results secretary and usually a trouble-shooter in case of emergency. The bulk of the responsibility for the main organisation of any meeting, in the weeks preceding the event, falls to the secretary of the meeting. It is a far from easy post, which requires a tremendous amount of enthusiasm, many hours of hard work, and above all a sense of humour and the ability to turn the other cheek at times when the going gets rough, as it undoubtedly will at times. Although many of the decisions will be made by the committee, it is easier at times to delegate the responsibilities for various phases of the organisation to the selected chiefs, who basically will attend to their own particular facet of the pre-event preparations.

The secretary of the meeting

The secretary of the meeting, as we have said, is almost certainly the main cog in the machinery of the organisation of any meeting. His work begins shortly after the first committee meeting. At the first meeting, the committee will have decided the format of the meeting, and the various classes will have been selected as well as the status of the event. It could be that the meeting will be for just members of the organising club, or in other words a closed-to-club meeting, or it could be restricted to the organising club and certain invited motor sporting clubs. If it is a championship qualifying event, which would have been decided at the original dates meeting by invitation of the various championship organisers, then the meeting may be of a National status and open to basically any holder of an RAC competition licence. However, once the status of the event, the date and venue, the officials and the classes have been formulated, the secretary of the meeting can then prepare the regulations for the meeting, having also, via the committee, decided on the competitors entry fee. The latter again depends very much on the financial viability of the venue, with regard to spectators' admission charges and the whole financial scene in total, which will have been carefully budgeted with the help of the committee. The regulations, once printed, are then distributed to drivers, a now costly process involving a tremendous amount of postal charges. Often the fact that the meeting regulations are available will be advertised in the motor sporting press, bringing a wealth of enquiries from prospective competitors. A copy of the regulations is also sent to the RAC with an application for a permit to run the meeting, usually in the case of an established club or venue, a formality.

The regulations will state the maximum permitted number of entries which will be accepted for the event, another decision which must be discussed carefully at the committee stage. It is extremely important to conclude the meeting at a reasonable hour, especially as many competitors may be travelling a long way to compete and will not wish to be late in making their way home. Whilst the regulations are being distributed the secretary of the meeting is kept extremely busy organising other sides of the event such as medical staff, in case of emergency, a public address system, a knowledgeable commentator, various caravans, possibly to house the officials on the day, RAC officials, such as timekeepers and scrutineers, with assistants, often such equipment as spectator barriers and fences and catering arrangements. Once the entries begin to flood in the secretary really cannot afford to relax, for initially, each entry application must be acknowledged, although at this point not necessarily accepted. As soon as the closing date for the entries for the meeting is reached, the secretary will, along with various other members of the committee, vet the applications received and in the case of the entry being oversubscribed decide which competitors regretfully will be refused an entry. Although no organiser likes to refuse entries, the original maximum number of starters must be adhered to, for if this is exceeded, it virtually without exception, leads to problems on the day, with a shortage of time. Hopefully, by the time that the entry list closes, the permit for the event will have been received from the RAC, along with the name of the steward who will attend the meeting on behalf of the RAC, to make sure that all runs smoothly. Once the entry list has been formulated, the final instructions are printed with details of the competitors' competition number, all the times of the events, and other relevant information including any changes which may have come about since the printing of the original regulations. The unsuccessful competitors are also informed, and of course their entry fee is refunded.

With the final regulations in the post the thoughts now turn to the programme for the event, and it is the secretary of the meeting who often will design it, which hopefully will include not only the classes and the entry list for the meeting, but also additional information which should prove of interest to the spectators. Once the programme is ready, it is forwarded to the printer with an order for the appropriate number of copies, dependent on the anticipated crowd. Also at this point, the press and publicity officer will be brought into the act, for he will have by now obtained some advertising to help pay for the programme printing costs, and will also require details of the entry for the meeting, to carry out a publicity campaign. Although the secretary of the meeting should now in theory be able to relax until the morning of the event, there are always numerous problems which crop up.

However, hopefully the next item in the secretary's agenda will be the signing-on of competitors on the special RAC sheet. All competitors at the meeting must sign this sheet for insurance purposes. Once all the signing-on is completed, and this usually provides little in the way of problems, the secretary can then inform the other officials of the meeting of any non arrivals, who can be officially listed as non-starters. Then his job is basically complete, although as always there will be queries and the few occasional problems. Once the meeting is completed the secretary still has a few tasks to perform in the coming week, for he must send a copy of the results to the RAC along with the fees for the meeting and the insurance cover, which is a pro rata rate based on the number of competitors. All that then remains is the accounts, for having often paid the RAC officials and various other contractors, such as the public address suppliers, on the day, there are still the programmes to be paid for as well as a host of other incidental expenses, such as the hire of the course. Once settled, the treasurer of the club can at last formulate a balance sheet which hopefully will show a small profit.

As you can see the work carried out by the secretary of the meeting is indeed exacting, and often an assistant is appointed to help out with many of the smaller jobs such as addressing envelopes and duplicating the regulations, the final instructions and results.

The clerk of the course

It is the clerk of the course who is responsible for the smooth running of the meeting on the track. Again this post is not only at times a very exacting one, but also a most responsible position. The timings of the meeting will have been worked out at an earlier committee meeting, for inclusion in the final instructions to competitors, and it is vital that sufficient time be left between the practice and the competition runs to allow the hard working club members a sufficient lunch break. Time must also be allowed for incidents, which hopefully may never happen, but should they occur they can often be time consuming and throw a meeting way behind schedule. The clerk of the course, along with his assistant, and often the chief marshal, will visit the course several times before the meeting, to decide the position of straw bales and barriers. This is a very important task for, as we have mentioned before, a hillclimb in particular, almost invariably has solid obstacles often within inches of the edge of the track, and these must be padded to avoid severe damage to a competing car and driver, should it leave the course at high speed. The clerk of the course will organise sufficient straw bales, spectator fences and ropes, and will usually spend at least a day at the venue in the week preceding the event in order to make sure that all the safety precautions are correct. There is no point whatsoever in taking short cuts, as the RAC steward will inspect the course before the event, and only when he is satisfied that everything is in order will the practice commence.

During his visits to the course, the clerk of the course will liase with both the chief course and paddock marshals, and the marshalling points will be decided, as well as the allocation of such equipment as asbestos blankets and fire extinguishers. The course communications system will be tried and tested, and a course controller appointed to take charge of the master telephone, which will be connected to all marshalling points on the course. The clerk of the course, having satisfied himself and the RAC steward, that the track is ready will then see that the practice for the event gets away on time. Barring any incidents he could well have a relatively quiet day.

However, should an incident of note occur on the track, it is his responsibility to attend, quite often with the RAC steward, to ascertain the problem at first hand, and instigate a swift return to the competition. Should medical attention be required for a driver, the course controller will receive the message from the appropriate marshalling point, and will immediately put out a call on the track communications system to the doctor and the ambulances, which will be positioned at an appropriately selected spot by the clerk of the course. In addition to caring for the safety angle of the event, the clerk of the course must also deal with any protests that may arise out of the conduct of the meeting, and this requires, at times, more than a small amount of tact. Although an official protest must be made in writing, with an appropriate protest fee, it is seldom, if ever, taken up in hillclimbing and sprinting, for the clerk of the course will sooothe frayed tempers and prevent an official protest.

The lot of a clerk of the course can be a frantic one, particularly if things begin to go wrong on the track. Certainly this position would not fall to an inexperienced organiser, but such is the honour of holding this post, that it can be generally the most sought after position amongst organisers, and certainly on the day it is a most responsible one.

Chief marshals

For most speed events, the organising committee will appoint two chief marshals, who will liase closely with the clerk of the course. The first chief marshal will be in control of the actual course marshals. It is his job to recruit sufficient manpower to adequately staff the course, with, preferably some spare men in case of emergency. The clerk of the course, in conjunction with the chief course marshal, will decide the various points on the course which will need manning, and the number of marshals per post. The chief course marshal will often also be responsible for the equipment which is required at each post. This includes a red flag for stopping approaching competitors in the case of an emergency, a fire extinguisher, an asbestos blanket, and often a grappling hook, which may be necessary in the case of a serious accident. Although there are usually fully equipped rescue vehicles with cutting equipment on the course, they can often take a minute or so to reach the incident, and often quick action by a marshal can save serious injury to a driver. It is the marshal who is the mainstay of the meeting, for the job is especially difficult, and often calls for long hours, sometimes in appalling conditions. It is the special job of the chief course marshal to make sure that his marshals stay on the ball, for they are always the first link in the emergency services, and must be obviously alert. Many chief marshals will manage to recruit a surplus of marshals, which means that he can operate a rota system, allowing the marshals a break from their posts without disrupting the meeting. The chief marshal, on the day of the event, will not remain at one post, but will travel up and down the course, making sure that all is well with his men (and women), quickly sorting out any staffing problems which might arise.

The chief paddock marshal is one on whom the smooth running of the meeting depends, for it is his job to ensure that the competitors come to the start line in their correct order, when required. In the days preceding the meeting, the chief paddock marshal, along with other members of the organising staff and his own assistants, will lay out the paddock with the competitors' numbers. This will be arranged to ensure a smooth flow to the paddock exit, and back into the paddock as the competitors return en masse after their runs. The paddock marshals must be on duty bright and early at the start of the day, to ensure that the arriving competitors park in the appropriate spaces, and must maintain the upper hand throughout the meeting. Without a semi-military-like precision, the paddock area and the whole running of the meeting can quickly degenerate into chaos, so once again firmness with a little tact is the order of the day.

Press, publicity and public relations officer

The role of press, publicity and public relations officer, is an extremely important one in the organisation of a meeting. Often a knowledgeable approach to the whole business of marketing an event to the general public can amount in a fair profit, rather than a loss. The first job undertaken by the publicity officer is the accumulation of advertising for the programme, in itself a far from easy task. A good man for the job will actually go a step further and attempt to obtain a sponsor for the event, usually a local businessman who must be persuaded that he can really benefit by injecting some cash into the meeting. Obviously this is a difficult task, but with an enthusiastic publicity officer, who can offer various advertising and promotional ideas which can be incorporated into the meeting, it is possible to achieve this source of extra revenue, which as will be shown later, can well provide the backer with a more than acceptable return for his investment. Once the programme advertisers are organised, ideally well before the programme goes to print, the next stage in the promotional task is to carry out a pre-meeting advertising campaign. This must be thoroughly costed in conjunction with the whole of the organising committee. Once the method of marketing is decided, and this is sure to include posters and car stickers, it is vital that the advertising media be bright and attractive, and carry the message well, and are not just absorbed into the background and overlooked by the public. It may be, if the meeting is a large one, that the club may sanction a series of television advertisements, but this can be costly and again must be very carefully programmed to carry the maximum impact for the minimum of expenditure.

However, even if television advertising is ruled out, and for the majority of clubs this is the case, it is usually possible to generate interest amongst the local newspapers, especially if a little advertising space is taken. The publicity officer, with a little work, can generally, coupled with the advertising, persuade the local newspapers to carry a feature article on the event in the week preceding the competition, often with photographs. The local radio and television stations can also usually be persuaded to give pre-event coverage. It is important that the press officer informs the national motoring press of the event, as they will usually carry a preview article, and often will send one of their local reporters to cover the event for the following week's edition. Press passes should be sent to all interested parties such as local newspapers, television and radio stations, as well as the motoring press.

With the almost cost free help from such organisations, plus the local advertising campaign, it should be possible to attract a good crowd, but the publicity officer should not rest on his laurels at the sight of a good crowd. He should make himself available to the local and national reporters who may be covering the event, giving them every assistance, for good post-event publicity will auger well for the next event. Should the press not send their own representative, the publicity officer would be required to furnish reports to the absent parties, in the hope that they might use them. If they do not, this should not deter the club from following the same course for the next event, for with an increasing amount of sport now available, it is difficult, even for the most sport conscious editor, to carry reports of every event. The publicity officer can be very hardworking, and should normally possess knowledge of the sport beyond local level, for authoritive pre-event information, with a good build-up, can be the way to large crowds and increased revenue.

Chief spectator marshal

It is of vital importance that once the spectators have entered the venue, they are able to watch the proceedings with as good a view as the course can give. It is here that the chief spectator marshal comes into his own, for with liason with the clerk of the course, the spectator areas can be prepared to the greatest advantage. The chief spectator marshal will organise what could well be a very large team to assist him. It is imperative that spectators, and indeed their cars, are not held up in long queues, and so the car parking arrangements, coupled with the taking of the gate money, and the selling of the programmes, must be a slickly well organised exercise. The chief spectator marshal would liase with the treasurer of the motor club to obtain the admission tickets, which of course must be especially printed to include a special 'motor racing is dangerous' rider. Also he should supply an adequate number of programmes, as well as the all important loose change float.

As with the track marshals, the spectator marshals, particularly on the admission gates, should be relieved frequently, as it is a wearing job, whilst along the course the chief marshal will install travelling spectator marshals to ensure that the public do not encroach on the prohibited areas at the trackside. Only officials of the meeting who have signed the chief marshal's RAC signing-on sheet are permitted onto the trackside, due to the insurance restrictions which must be adhered to. At the end of the day, the chief spectator marshal will accumulate the gate takings, and will usually, the day after the meeting, count the proceeds, and present the total to the club treasurer who will then work out a balance sheet for the event, once all the bills have been presented by the secretary of the meeting.

The results secretary

As the meeting progresses, the timekeepers will produce a list of times for each batch of competitors, which will then be sent to the results secretary who will enter them on a stencil of the entry list, prepared in advance. As the times are known, and the various class competitions are completed, the results of each class will be worked out, and this will also be typed on the stencil. At the end of the day, the completed stencils are duplicated, thus providing an almost instant results service, for competitors and press alike. However, there are often competitors who, having completed their day's sport, head for home before the end of the meeting, and the production of the results sheets, and it is the responsibility of the results secretary to see that every competitor receives a full set of results. These must be posted in the coming week, as will the RAC copies, and the copies supplied by the press officer to the media who were not represented at the meeting.

Club stewards

The club stewards are appointed by the organising club, basically to help sort out any queries which might arise as to the conduct of the meeting. There could, for instance, be a halfhearted protest by a competitor, and rather than involve the clerk of the course, and the RAC steward, the club stewards can usually pour oil on the troubled waters. Basically, the club stewards double as trouble-shooters, although it is always a good idea to allocate a competent person to act as the latter, should any small incidents arise. The trouble-shooter can, as his name implies, be actively employed in any area of the event, to sort out minor problems as they arise, but again this should be an experienced sprint or hillclimb man with a fair knowledge of the business.

Commentator

There are, of course, many other people within a motor club who go to make up a successful event, but worthy of a mention must be the commentator, for it is he who is the direct link between the public and the event. With spectators paying to view the competition, it is always a good idea to employ a commentator who is a specialist, rather than a local club man who may know the local contingent, but be out of touch with the visitors from further afield. The job of commentating is not easy, especially if there is a delay, for it is imperative that the spectators do not become bored, and hence disinterested. In such a case, and no matter how good the organisation, it can happen that the commentator is the only man who can keep the customer satisfied. The sport of hillclimb and sprinting is a closely contested one, whether in the saloon car class or amongst the larger and extremely rapid racing cars, but with an out-of-touch commentator, this is lost to the general public.

Hillclimbing and sprinting, just like the cinema or theatre, is an entertainment, and must be treated as such. There is no doubt that it is a specialised sport and it therefore requires a very specialised knowledge to impart the same enthusiasm to the general public, which is generated by the people within the sport. This can only be achieved by a knowledgeable and competent commentator, and if the organising club does not have such a person, it is a worthwhile investment to import such a specialist, even if it costs a small amount to do so.

9 You can do it in a home built car

Even to the many thousands of people within sprinting and hillclimbing, there is a feeling that it is not possible to contest a national championship without a great deal of expense, and a purpose built machine. Although in terms of the RAC Hillclimb Championship, this is true, it is possible to prove highly competitive in some of the other series, without a bottomless bank balance. It has been proved in the past by several drivers. Let us take a look at one such competitor, Cheltenham driver Alan Richards, who in 1975 dominated the RAC/ Woking Motors Ltd Leaders Hillclimb Championship with his home built and prepared, Gryphon 3AR single seater racing car. The Leaders championship, unlike the main RAC series itself, is contested on a class basis rather than by an outright fastest time, and so, therefore, it was necessary to produce a car which was capable of winning its own particular class at each event. This was finally achieved with the Gryphon, but it was not an easy process by any means, for as in any sport, success is only achieved by dedication to the task in hand, a will to win, and a tremendous amount of hard work. To really appreciate the achievements of Alan, his brother-in-law Graham Garbutt, who helped to prepare the car, and the Gryphon itself, we have to delve back into the almost dark, distant past, and really start from the beginning.

Being a Cheltenham lad, and right on the doorstep of the fabulous Prescott Hillclimb, it was not unnatural for Alan to take an interest in hillclimbing when he was in his early twenties. He seldom missed the chance of visiting the superb Gloucestershire hill to take in the unique hillclimb atmosphere, watch the maestros of the day in action, and almost immediately the desire to compete was born, but like many younger people, there was no cash available to buy a competitive car, and enter the fray. However, in those days the Bugatti Owners Club, who organise the Prescott meetings, would stage an open practice day for allcomers, and the temptation to try his skills on a real hillclimb was too much to resist; so Alan, complete with his road going A35, took the opportunity to try his luck. The day finished with almost total disillusionment, as his times, despite some apparently frantic efforts, were just not what he had hoped for, but he knew there was more to come. It was obvious that the road going A35 was not suitable for hillclimbing, and so after a period of drastic saving, the first competition car was purchased. In Alan's own words "A disaster called the Halden JAP." This was a little rear engined motorcycle engine propelled single seater racing car, which hopefully, was going to provide Alan with his first real taste of hillclimbing. However as they say "The best laid plans of mice and men ..." was an apt phrase, for having bought the car, it was decided, before entering it in a competition, to give it a short run down the road, (not to be recommended), to make sure that everything was in working order. After a tremendous amount of pushing and shoving the little beast finally burst into life, and took off down the public highway.

It worked, and the elation was almost unbelievable. The elation soon turned to gloom and despondency, for just a quarter of a mile down the road, the carburettor almost fell off, causing a minor fire at the back of the car. However, a local resident came to the rescue, and threw a door mat over the blaze, followed by handfuls of earth. It certainly put the fire out, but also meant a trip back to the workshop to clean down the car and attend to the problems. Despite the close proximity of the local Chief Constable's house, further illegal tests were carried out on the road, and gradually, the car began to look and sound like a racer. It was becoming quite fleet of foot for having passed the Chief Constable's house, it was always a mad panic to get the car back to the safety of the garage before the local Panda car appeared. Somehow, despite the temperamental nature of the Halden, this was always achieved, and eventually the big day came. Its first real meeting, a sprint, passed off with little success, but also fortunately no major disasters. Having taken part in a few more sprints, it was time to graduate to the hills, and not surprisingly the venue was Prescott. It is always the ambition of any car and driver to make a lasting impression on his colleagues, on his first appearance, and Alan did just that, but not in the way intended. The car split its gearbox wide open on the start line, depositing a *Torre Canyon*-like slick of oil, and that was enough for Alan. The car was then disposed of, although its memories will last in the mind of the driver for many years to come.

After a couple of years to recover from the disasters of the Halden, which included numerous engine blow ups, Alan again took up the cudgels of competition, using his road going MGB. This did not really prove to be competitive, although it again whetted his appetite to go hillclimbing and sprinting, and led to a partnership being formed with Mike Bolton. It led further to the purchase of the remarkably named Alter Ego Special which was built to the monoposto formula. It was originally fitted with a Fiat engine, and incredibly, a Citroen Light 15 gearbox. The car, however, was acquired without the engine, and so for the princely sum of £75, a well modified Ford Anglia engine was purchased. However, before inserting the engine, the car was completely stripped and rebuilt, and then renamed the Gryphon, appearing for the first time in its new form at the Long Marston sprint. Much to the delight of everyone, Alan took a fine second in class, beaten only by the 1500cc Rudeani of Jack Heaton Rudd, a very experienced competitor. After the success at Long Marston, several other events were attempted with the one litre car during the rest of the season.

The earlier encouraging result could not be repeated, and with a quick check over during the winter, the new season opened again at Prescott, and would you believe it, the car broke its gearbox on the start line. Now, as you will remember, the gearbox was based on a Citroen Light 15 unit, and this would usually have been a problem to replace, but for once, luck was on Alan's side, and he located a complete car for sale in a local garage, unbelievably just three miles from Prescott. After much haggling and wrangling, the whole car was purchased for the vast amount of £15, and rushed home along with the Gryphon. An all night rebuilding session on the gearbox saw the car on the start line at Prescott the next day, and for once Alan and Mike were rewarded for their dedication, with Mike taking a heartwarming second place in his class.

After the Prescott meeting, it was decided to try and modify the bodywork, the boys' first efforts at glassfibre work, but the result was pleasing, and the car looked extremely similar to the Eagle Formula One Grand Prix car. With the car now finished in metallic blue, it was beginning to look extremely attractive, but the one big problem was still the handling, for the chassis was far from one of the best, and at the end of the year Mike was unfortunate enough to roll the car at the Woburn Hillclimb. Although he emerged virtually unhurt, the car was in a sad state. Fortunately with winter again approaching, there was plenty of time for Alan and Mike to rebuild the car, and this was achieved in time for the start of the new season, but still the handling was far from good, and following an accident at the Pontypool Hillclimb, Mike decided to take no further part in the venture, leaving Alan to go it alone. Following the contact with a tree at Pontypool, the chassis was again in a sad state, and so Alan and his brother-in-law Graham completely stripped the main components of the car, and a complete rebuild was undertaken, at the same time the front suspension being completely redesigned and built by Alan. When the car reappeared later in the season, it was certainly better than ever before, and started to show a great deal of potential. However, to a perfectionist like Alan, the car was still in need of development, and it was the rear suspension which was then redesigned, and this proved to be the answer. The car in Alan's hands immediately became one of the pacemakers in the up to 1100cc racing car class, and took five class wins, whilst the season was rounded off in the best possible way with an outright fastest time of the day at Fairford Sprint.

Despite the influx of success, Alan, like most competitive racing drivers, felt that he needed more power, and with the chassis now apparently capable of handling additional horsepower, it was the next step. But which was the way to go? The up to 1100cc racing car class had seen the Ford MAE Formula 3 engine and the full race Hillman Imp engine more than making their impression amongst the potential class winning cars, but Alan was most intrigued by the idea of supercharging the existing engine. When the chance of a supercharger for just £50 came along, the decision was taken, and the winter was spent grafting the new power booster onto the existing engine. However, when the car appeared at the start of the season, it was back to the days of the Halden JAP, as one disaster followed another. The engine just did not prove strong enough to take the additional boost supplied by the supercharger and was constantly blowing cylinder head gaskets, whilst the drive to the supercharger also

Champion Year: Alan Richards
with the Cheltenham Cameras
sponsored Gryphon 3AR en
route to the RAC Leaders
Hillclimb Championship

Hillclimbing and sprinting tends to bring out the best in experimentation, such as this
supercharged Ford engined Morris Minor which has proved a most rapid car in the hands of
Trevor King

The incredible Voigt-Konig, the
car built by Peter Voigt which
aided by the high revving Konig
outboard motor engine, proved
an incredible success in the up to
500cc racing car class, taking
overall victory in the BARC
Hillclimb Championship. Voigt
sold the car to David Fyfe, the
Scottish driver, who is seen here
flinging the car into Radio Corner
at Bouley Bay

proved a sore point with belts breaking and flying off the pulleys at every meeting. The engine was also fitted with an ultra light flywheel, and this made the car totally uncontrollable, as the power would only come-in viciously, and with the necessary smoothness not on hand, spins and excursions were the order of the day. The car progressed along the track in a manner akin to a kangaroo in full flight. Despite these problems Alan persevered with the car and fitted the fashionable rear aerofoil and front fins, in an effort to improve the handling of the car at high speed. Although success was hard to come by, there was a glorious few minutes at Shelsley Walsh when Alan actually broke the class record, only to see Roger Willoughby snatch it back with his Brabham a few moments later. Towards the end of the season, the inevitable happened, and the engine cried enough, blowing itself into a thousand little pieces. Now it really was back to the drawing board.

The result of the engine blow-up forced Alan to obtain a secondhand block along with other spares, and a new engine was built up. The experiences and failures of the past seasons had to be taken into account. With no testing facilities available, the car was taken to a local factory car park to run for the first time, and although it seemed to be much better than the old unit, unbeknown to Alan and Graham, a stone had found its way into the engine via the carburettor. This did not show up at the test session, but all was revealed at the first meeting as the engine began to make death knell noises. With the internal parts of the motor in a sad state, another rebuild was called for. This proved far more successful, although a head gasket problem still reared its head from time to time, and whilst the Ford Motor Company rubbed its hands in glee at the thought of extra spares turn-over, the problem just had to be solved. It was, by the acquisition of a new cylinder head. This proved a major turning point in the career of Alan and the Gryphon, for from then on the pair proved extremely competitive, and although they did not concentrate on the Leaders Hillclimb Championship, their success rate was such that they finished sixth overall in the series and broke class records at Penrice, Shelsley Walsh and Weston Speed Trials. They also became the fastest home built supercharged car ever to climb the historic Shelsley Hill, a tremendous achievement in itself.

The story of the success in the 1975 RAC/Woking Motors Ltd Leaders Hillclimb Championship is almost a fairy tale ending to several seasons of frustration and near despair. With 1974 successfully behind them and with the frivolities of a New Year's party not more than a few hours since departed, the first day of the year saw the decision taken to contest the championship seriously, at the expense of other events if need be. The year did not start well, for a temperamental motor coupled with a near spin and shortage of fuel, saw Alan and the Gryphon well beaten in the first round of the series at Loton Park. He then hit top form, and really did become the man to beat, as he took one championship win after another. After the misfortunes of previous years lady luck also smiled on the pair for the first time, and a chance meeting with George Gilbert, the managing director of Cheltenham Cameras, led to a sponsorship deal being agreed, the car being rechristened the Chelcam Gryphon. Despite the fact that the first meeting under the sponsor's banner resulted in a non-start due to engine problems, the pair quickly reasserted themselves at the head of their class, and at the top of the championship table. They looked like being on the way to taking the National title until disaster struck at Pontypool, where the car was forced to non-start due to engine problems. However Cheltenham driver Sandy Hutcheon came to the rescue, and kindly offered Alan a drive in his Ginetta. Alan replied by astonishing everyone, winning the class in the borrowed car. It was back to the Gryphon for the next rounds, and success continued, with only Harewood exponent John Crowson really being able to stop the all-conquering pair, when they visited the Yorkshire hill. By three quarters of the way through the season the title was theirs.

As you can see Alan Richards' path to a National championship victory has not been an easy one, but then such a challenge never is. He has, however, proved the point that it can be done in a home built car. Although he has certainly suffered engine and chassis problems, which could have proved frantically expensive, the cost of the rebuilds has been radically reduced by carrying out as much work as possible himself, and certainly his expenditure has been minimal compared with some competitors. Eventually the success rate was good only due to effort and enthusiasm, but then that is the stuff that hillclimbers and sprinters are made of.

Home built competition cars come in many shapes and sizes. This fearsome Channel Islands beast is powered by a Jaguar engine

Having successfully campaigned a Terrapin for several years, John Frampton engineered and built this Sphinx BMC, which also proved to be a very good car in the up to 1100cc racing car class

10 Sponsorship

Both hillclimbing and sprinting in Great Britain, just like most other forms of recreation, has suffered the ravages of inflation during the last few years. There is no doubt that the struggle to maintain competitive cars and stage good events has become a problem, with both competitors and organisers alike. Fortunately the influx of sponsorship into the sport has helped considerably. Firstly, let us define sponsorship. Basically, it is the injection of cash by a business, in return for advertising and promotion. Properly handled, this can be of great benefit to competitors, organisers and businessmen. Basically, there are three types of sponsorship; support for an individual car and driver, support for an individual meeting, or possibly a club, and the backing of a series of events such as an important championship series.

As the average hillclimb and sprint competitor in this country is a normal working individual, it is he or she, above all others, who have felt the escalating cost of competing weekly. It is the aim of virtually every competitor to land a sponsorship deal, but with even the larger companies cutting down on their advertising budget, this is not an easy task. Certainly of all the competitors who attempt to organise sponsorship, only a small minority are successful. To obtain financial assistance from a company, one must be prepared in return to devote some time and effort into waving the company banner in a way which will achieve additional company interest, and bring their particular product to the eye of the general public. There are many benefits to a company who are prepared to become involved in hillclimbing and sprinting, but firstly they will basically only be interested in a reasonably successful competitor, who has in the past achieved a modicum of success, for it is the pacemakers in the class that really attract the attentions of the spectators. Once a sponsorship deal has been agreed with a company, it usually requires that the competition car be resprayed in company colours with the maximum amount of advertising space devoted to the company and their product. This should be tastefully carried out with a special eye to making the car attractive, whether it be on or off the course. Surprisingly a competing car on a trailer can cause a tremendous amount of attention as it travels on the public highway, so the car, wherever possible, should remain in full view of the public as the advertising potential for a business is almost as great away from the meeting, as it is on the course. Once at a meeting, it is often possible to arrange with the organisers for the display of company banners at trackside, and if possible, depending on the company's product, it may be possible for the general public to be handed out free samples or leaflets describing the company's area of business. It is a well known fact that motor sporting people are basically very patriotic. It has been proved in the past, that sponsorship, in the hands of the right competitor is definitely an excellent medium for boosting company sales, amongst not only the hillclimb and sprint fraternity, but also the members of the general public who will talk of a meeting long after most competitors have forgotten it. An attractively displayed advertising campaign on the side of a memorable car, will certainly make its impression.

The second form of sponsorship comes with the support of a company at an individual meeting. This usually involves a company who will trade in close proximity to the venue itself. Again, the main aim of the deal is to provide the club with a cash influx to help with the ever increasing cost of organising a meeting. A single meeting sponsorship, particularly with a local business involved, can be extremely beneficial to the organisers, especially in their pre event publicity. At the meeting itself, it is normal for the company to represent themselves with, possibly, a display of their wares in the paddock or spectator enclosures, whilst again, trackside advertising will be very much in evidence. The programme, naturally, will carry not only a message of thanks to the sponsor, for without him the meeting may well not have taken place, but also attractive advertising. It is essential that the general public and, indeed, the competitors and followers of the sport are made fully aware of the involvement of the sponsor. This can always be executed by the commentator, who again, becomes a very important link in keeping the meeting viable. In general, sponsorship of local meetings proves extremely worthwhile for the local businessman.

To a large and often national company, it is often of great benefit to sponsor a complete championship series, for this can give the company and their product coverage at as many as fifteen meetings throughout Great Britain during the year. It obviously costs a considerable amount more to support a complete championship series. Often the series will take the sponsor's name, as does the Guyson/BARC Hillclimb Championship, so thus Guyson, who support the series, are getting the company name into the newspapers weekly.* It is usual for a representative of the supporting company to attend the majority of the rounds which his company is supporting, and it is he who can really assure that the company develop the full advertising potential from the cash support which they are injecting. There will, undoubtedly, be regular press releases, and usually the programme for each meeting will carry an article with regard to the company and their wares. By the end of the year, if the campaign is properly organised, there will be few people who have attended an event of the series who will not know the full details of the sponsor and his business. With thousands of people attending sprints and hillclimbs weekly, this can only result in increased business and hopefully a profit on the investment, which is of course the aim of any company.

Although sponsorship is relatively new to sprinting and hillclimbing, it has already proved to be a very satisfactory advertising medium, and will undoubtedly flourish as long as the recipients of the help are prepared to reciprocate and promote the company.

The tension shows as Malcolm Dungworth waits for his next run

*Footnote: The publisher of this book is currently sponsoring the National sprint championship as it did in 1976. That championship is therefore called The Haynes Publishing RAC National Sprint Championship.

11 The fun in between

Although the business of championship hillclimbing calls for extreme dedication to the task in hand, a tremendous amount of physical and mental effort and a near professional approach from the drivers who regularly contend the prestigious and demanding events, there is still time for a very active social side. With the larger hillclimbs, in particular, attracting as many as one hundred and fifty competitors to a championship qualifying event, many travelling several hundreds of miles to compete, it is now often impossible to run such a highly supported meeting in just one day. It is becoming increasingly the accepted rule to run the practice for the event on the Saturday, whilst the event itself takes place on the Sunday, with just a small amount of practice on the morning of the competition. The majority of the competitors will practice on the Saturday and this does mean that a certain camaraderie develops between them. There are more and more social events taking place on the evening following practice, where the wives and children can get together, whilst the drivers can use the evening to unwind and prepare for the following day's combat. However, such is the nature of the average hillclimber and sprinter that these social get togethers on a Saturday evening invariably turn into a sparring contest of some kind or another, for the competitive instinct of the driver just fails to rest.

Whilst some organisers have now realised the value of the Saturday evening get together, and stage barbecues and discos, there are still many venues where no entertainment as such is supplied and often this is soon remedied. It is during these evenings that the hillclimber really comes into his own, and it is not unusual for an impromptu cricket match to be organised in the paddock, and although they always start in a semi-serious manner they quickly degenerate into a fabulous free for all. It is surprising how many of the ultra competitive drivers enjoy these tension breaking matches. The sight of Roy Lane, the 1975 and 1976 RAC Hillclimb champion, battling in the impromptu cricket match at Gurston would do credit to any Charlie Chaplin film, whilst his doctoring of the injured cricket bat, with a splint and masking tape, would do justice to any surgeon.

However, it is not just cricket matches which provide the entertainment and mirth, and not all the activities are exactly the safest in the world. For instance there was the monkey bike leaping contest at Doune where the main aim was to see how far you could fly through the air on a 50cc motorcycle. The rules stated you should not be separated from the machine, but these were quickly overlooked, whilst perhaps the most strenuous exercise to date has been the cycle race at Prescott, a climb of the full eleven hundred yard hill which left everyone except former cycle racing champion Roy Lane and Brabham driver John Hart, gasping for breath.

The social atmosphere at an overnight stop is always excellent, for with most competitors now equipped with caravans, motorhomes or tents, the little commune flourishes, often until the early hours of the morning, with its own brand of entertainment. Groups assemble and partake in a little light refreshment, whilst the usual amount of friendly teasing abounds. This is in complete contrast to the attitude of a driver just a few hours later as he seriously prepares for the task in hand, the battle between himself, his car and that unbeatable enemy, the clock.

Hillclimbing is fun. Roy Lane enjoys himself as he investigates the Palliser Repco of David Fyfe and Alex Brown

It can even be fun changing spark plugs on a V8 engined racing car, at least, it is for David Fyfe

12 Transporting the beast and equipment for racing

Once you have acquired a car, with which to compete at hillclimb and sprint events, the next problem is the transportation to and from the courses. It may be, to begin with, that you have decided to use your own road going car, and this presents no problem at all, as you simply drive the car to the event, remove a few of the superfluous trims such as wheel embellishers, tape over the headlights and take part in the competition. However, once the attraction of sprinting and hillclimbing has taken its hold on you, it is almost inevitable that the next stage will be a car prepared to full racing specification. Hence even if this is a saloon or sports car, it will be totally unsuitable for road use, and it is here that transportation problems can begin. The most common method of getting a racing car to a meeting is by the use of a trailer. There are many versions to choose from. The most popular type is the single axle version, and although these can often be purchased quite cheaply when secondhand, or even constructed at home with only a modest outlay, they do have their problems. Being just two wheeled they are not capable of carrying really heavy cars, but unless you are contesting the vintage class, or as in the case of the drivers of very potent single seater racing cars, carrying a variety of spare wheels and tyres as well as other spares, you will probably find that the weight of your racing equipe is well within the capabilities of the average two wheeled trailer. The main drawback is of course the 50 miles an hour speed limit, which can be irksome on long journeys.

The second alternative, and certainly a much better bet if you wish to carry a reasonable amount of weight, is the far more stable four wheeled trailer. On the whole, these are naturally quite expensive in comparison to the two wheeled versions, but they are far more robust, and heavier, thus requiring a reasonably sized tow car. They are possibly the most popular form of transportation for racing cars, especially as certain models can legally be towed on the motorway at 70 miles per hour, although they are banned from the outside lane of the three carriageway systems. One word of warning however, the law regarding 70 mile per hour travel with four wheeled close coupled trailers is complex, and when purchasing such a device, it is advised that the local police are consulted on its legal right to travel at the maximum permitted speed on a motorway.

With an increasing number of meetings requiring a two day attendance, it is not surprising to find an ever growing number of mobile homes being used to tow the trailer, for they can double as sleeping accommodation, and thus cut out the possible inconvenience of an hotel. The overnight stop has now led to a new trend in the transportation of racing vehicles to meetings, seeing a growth in the numbers of specially converted transporters appearing. Though at first glance, a purpose built transporter, which would be either based on a large box van lorry or a coach, might seem an expensive project, it does not necessarily follow. There are many competitors who are now converting their own coaches and lorries into, not only a transporter for the car, but also a mobile home, with the family able to enjoy all the comforts of a kitchen, dining area and adequate sleeping space. However, these conversions, with a few exceptions, are not professional conversions as the cost to the average competitor would be far too prohibitive. A well used coach or lorry is purchased by the competitor himself, who will then carry out the alterations and design a set up which will best suit his own personal requirements. Often,

Even the brutish McLaren M10B can be transported on a two wheel trailer

with careful choice of an older vehicle, this can be achieved for less than the price of an average saloon car, and with no trailer to worry about the motorway cruising speed is again the maximum permitted, seventy miles per hour.

The choice of tow cars and transporters is obviously one which can only be made by the person involved, but the transportation of the racing machine to a meeting is not a problem which can be solved only by heavy expenditure. Often the right choice of transportation can result in a great saving of money during the season, when items like hotel bills, fuel consumption and practicability are all taken into account, and the right decision reached.

Equipment for racing

Once the plunge has been taken, and the decision to start racing has been made, it is necessary to purchase some vital equipment, mainly in the interest of your own safety and personal comfort.

Crash helmet

Because the sport of hillclimbing and sprinting is purely a speed sport, it is vital that a good quality crash helmet be purchased and worn. Fortunately, the RAC who govern the sport, have laid down stringent regulations as to the standards of crash helmets which are permitted, and it is imperative that the crash helmet, when purchased, should be one which is acceptable to the RAC scrutineer who will check it prior to the meeting. There are, naturally, a wide selection of crash helmets to choose from, many of which are far from inexpensive, but it is one area where it does not pay to go for second best, for should you need the assistance of a crash helmet, you will want it to do its job, and protect you. It often pays to spend a little more and be sure. If you are in doubt, do not be afraid to ask the advice of your fellow competitors, who will be only too pleased to help you, and give you the benefit of their own personal experience.

The choice of a good crash helmet is often a personal one. Sir Nicholas Williamson prefers the type with a built in cigarette support

Vizor or goggles

If you are competing in a closed car, it will not be necessary to wear either goggles or a vizor, as you are protected from the wind, rain and dust, by the windscreen of the car, but if you are driving an open car, this is an essential part of your equipment. With the majority of the crash helmets now being of the fully enveloping type, it is usual to purchase a vizor, which is made especially to fit the appropriate helmet, and these are available in many forms, from clear type to dark tint. It may well be a good idea to purchase two vizors, one clear one and one tinted one, to combat the glare of the sun on a bright day. The modern vizors are all made of a high impact material, but should you decide to opt for the older style goggles, make sure that they are also not easily breakable, for if a stone should fly up from a front wheel, the goggles will be of no use to you if they shatter. They could well cause a serious accident. Again if in doubt about the suitability for the purpose, ask a person who knows.

Gloves

There are many excellent driving gloves on the market and the choice is a personal one. The one thing to watch is the palms, for they should not be glossy, and should allow a firm grip of the wheel.

Shoes

When driving at high speed, where a quick change from one pedal to the next is required, it is imperative that the soles of the shoes afford sufficient grip. Once again, there are some excellent driving shoes available at most motor accessory shops, but they are relatively expensive and many drivers opt for the far cheaper plimsol, or basketball type of boot, which generally seems to cope more than adequately with the task. They are, of course, available at any shoe shop for a small sum of money, although they are not flame resistant.

Driving overalls

It is highly recommended that before attempting a speed competition, a driver obtains a set of racing overalls which are custom designed for the sport. There are various types to choose from, ranging from a flameproof set right through the range to a semi-fireproof suit. These overalls have been specially designed with the fire hazard of an accident in mind, and even the cheaper suits can provide a limited protection against flames, whilst up to forty five seconds of protection against fire is provided by the more expensive suits. These can be used in conjunction with specially designed flame-resistant underwear, not a cheap kit, but again with human life at stake at times, a very worthwhile safety aid.

Roll-over bars

Having kitted yourself out with the appropriate driver safety devices, do not forget the car, for in the case of an accident thoughtful safety precautions can almost certainly save a great deal of personal injury. No matter what type of car you drive, a roll-over bar is essential for should the car turn over, the bar will absorb much of

Unfortunately not all accidents are minor. The remains of a Mini Cooper S resting in the undergrowth at Doune in a rather sorry state although the driver, due to an efficient roll over bar, emerged unscathed

the impact. Once again the RAC have laid down their own standards of acceptable bars, and these must be adhered to. They are not cheap, but can and usually do, save the driver from injury, as well as often reducing the damage to the motor car by a substantial margin, thus also saving money on the necessary repairs. Do not attempt to make your own roll-over bar unless you have specialist knowledge of the forces involved, and do not try to take short cuts with cheaper models, unless they have proved themselves. Remember your life is too valuable; safety first is always the motto in hillclimbing and sprinting.

Seat belts

Just as on the road in everyday life, the seat belt has proved a boon in preventing driver injury in the case of motor sport accidents. From experience, there can be little doubt that the only effective seat belt system is the full harness type which provides all round support to the body in an emergency. It is definitely not recommended that any other type of seat belt is used, as these have at times, proved ineffective when it really matters. No matter what type of seat belts are fitted, it is vital that they be securely fixed in a professional manner, for the anchorages take a tremendous strain in the event of an accident, a strain they can absorb only if fitted correctly in the first place. If a belt is subjected to stress during an accident, like its counterpart in a road car, it must be replaced and not re-used.

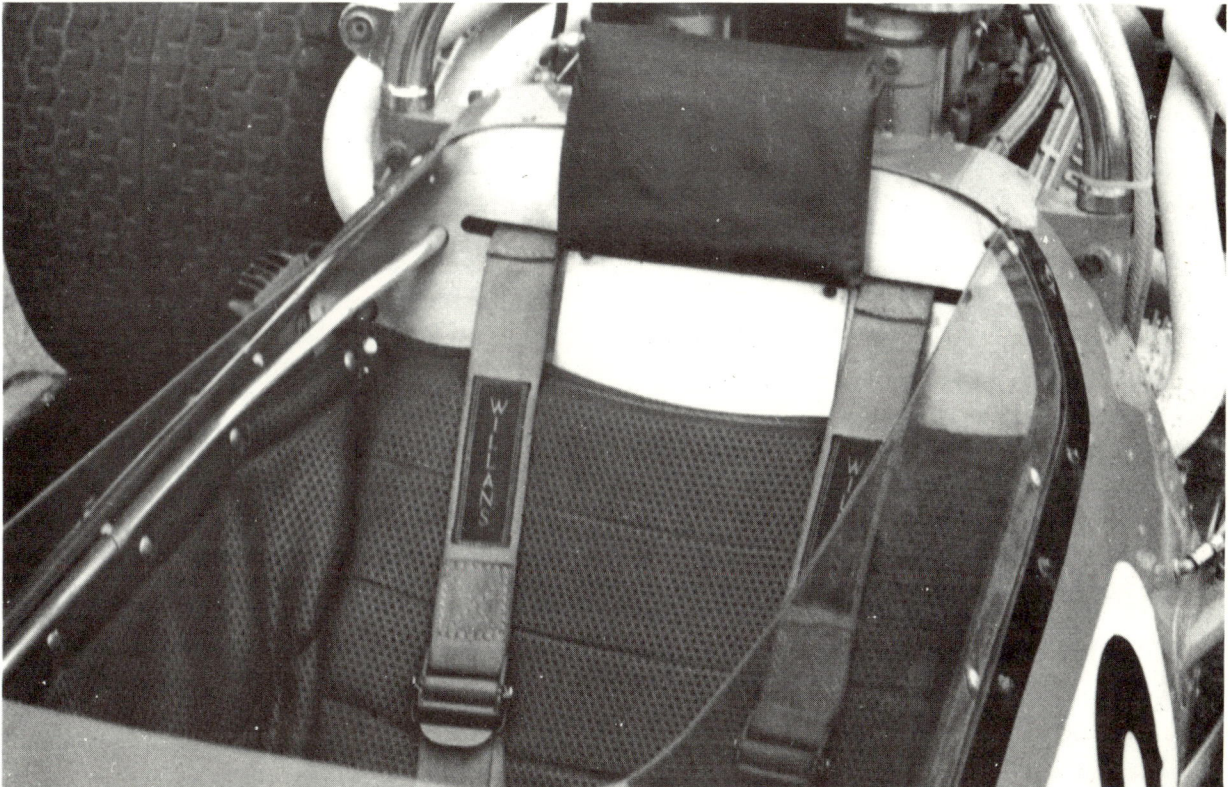

A most essential safety aid in the racing car is the full harness seat belt

Fire extinguisher

Although not compulsory at the time of writing, it is almost certain that in the course of time it will be mandatory for all competing cars to carry at least a two and a half pound dry power fire extinguisher. Again it makes sense to invest in such a device, for should for instance, an electrical fire occur, either during a run, or even in the paddock, it may well be a minute before the ever efficient fire marshals reach you, and in that time a considerable amount of damage can occur. If you have your own extinguisher, you may well avoid a great deal of this damage. In the case of many cars, and in particular single seater racing machines, it is now possible to kit the car with an automatic fire extinguisher, which will discharge upon impact with a solid object, and this of course is also fitted with a manual switch to allow discharge at any time when required. Again this can prove a tremendous help, and can often prevent serious damage in the case of a fire incident, as they are extremely efficient, although again far from inexpensive.

13 Come ride with me - a cockpit-eye view of a sprint

What is it really like to drive a highly powerful racing car in a competition? For the first time, well simply, frightening. Such a machine is well capable of biting back if abused, but above all there is a tremendous exhilaration as the back of the seat hits you when you stroke the throttle and plummet down the straight with almost unbelievable acceleration.

However, let us start at the beginning. It is the end of September, with the hillclimb and sprint season rapidly drawing to an end, and your hard working author is steadily ploughing his way through an incredible amount of boring and depressing paperwork in the office, whilst at the same time bemoaning the fact that the summer sport, which has provided so much entertainment, is rapidly making way for the dark and cold nights, and a period of winter hibernation. At the same time he is wondering if his stars, which had stated that something unusual would happen during the day, would for once prove correct. They never had in the past, except on the bad news front, and certainly that promised windfall which had been forecast had never materialised. Stop dreaming lad, get on with the work, back to the mountain of paperwork and the numerous telephone calls from customers querying accounts. Suddenly the telephone shrills away in the corner of the room, no don't throw the telephone directory at it, just answer it, after all it can only be just another problem. Having lifted the receiver, and answered with a reasonably happy sounding voice, well after all, all businessmen are good actors, I am immediately greeted with "What are you doing a fortnight on Sunday?" and recognise the voice of McLaren driver Dave Harris, the runner up in the 1974 RAC Sprint Championship and the champion in 1975 and 1976. "Nothing, we have finished the season after next weekend, and shall spend the whole day in bed probably." "Well, I'm doing the club sprint at Wroughton" quoth our happy go lucky racing driver, "Why don't you have a go?" Quick as a flash came back the usual reply, "What in?" "My McLaren" he said. Conversation ends momentarily in a deathly silence, could I really be hearing things, or is this the chance of a lifetime. No time to talk it over with my wife, "Right you're on," for no-one in their right mind could refuse an offer like that.

It was from then on that the problems really began, the first item on the agenda being to convince my wife, not an easy task, especially when the fastest car you have driven before is a BMW saloon. However, for once the astrologers were right, and luck was on my side for with my wife a little under the weather, she had agreed without really appreciating what I had said; stage one completed. The next problem was to rapidly obtain an RAC Competitions licence, and with the aid of a quick telephone call, and the speed of the postal service, this was arranged, whilst Dave had sent me an entry form for the meeting which was duly completed and sent to the secretary of the event. By this time it was too late to back out, even though for the week preceding the event, my legs felt as though they were made of jelly, and the thought of making a fool of myself in front of all the competitors I had spent the season writing about, was constantly going through my mind. Oh well, it will give them a chance to get their own back on me. The main worry during the week rested on the weather for I convinced myself thoroughly that the skies would open, which would only serve to make things even worse.

Eventually that fateful Sunday arrived after a typically sleepless night. It was not necessary to arise at such an early hour, a point echoed by my wife, but I was in such a tense state that all I wanted to do was get onto the road and head for the course. We had arranged to meet Dave at the venue at nine o'clock, and although it was only an hour's run up the motorway we left home at seven, taking the opportunity to cruise up the motorway, and convince ourselves that the weather looked reasonable and that rain was not in the air.

Upon arrival in the paddock we began the wait for Dave and the boys of Bath Street Garage with the McLaren. It seemed an eternity. Again severe doubts were going through my mind, but at last on the horizon a large red and white Ford Transit transporter appeared and just a couple of minutes later the equipe arrived in the paddock. After exchanging the customary morning greetings it was all hands to the pump and unload the car, a task rapidly achieved, and in no time it was at the scrutineering bay and passed fit for the event. Although practice by this time was underway there seemed no sense of urgency to venture out onto the circuit, and time was taken for a fitting in the car which provided immediate problems. Now your author is not amongst the smallest of people, and the first lesson of the day was how to get into the car, a feat achieved with a struggle, although it might have been easier with a large shoe horn. However, once settled into the beast it proved remarkably comfortable, and the pedals and the gear change all fell to hand quite easily. Time was then taken to explain the intricacies of the gear selection, for although the car was fitted with a five speed gearbox, first gear was not necessary, even when starting off. Fortunately this meant that with the start being made in second gear, the gear change was exactly the same as a normal road car.

The Wroughton course, being laid out on a large airfield, does mean that there is plenty of space to gently try a car prior to a run and so I took the opportunity of slowly driving the car to the end of the paddock road, in the process trying every gear change position, each of which was easily found. Returning to the transporter, it was time for Dave to take his first practice run, so whilst he prepared, I borrowed a crash hat from a local Mini driver, wrestled into Rob Turnbull's spare racing suit, which served only to make me feel like Tweedledum as Rob is considerably taller than I am, and certainly not as wide of girth. Having struggled into the suit, it was up to the paddock exit to watch Dave's first practice run. Now, with my own brother-in-law as the RAC timekeeper at the meeting, I was soon greeted with a shout of "92 seconds, beat that", followed by the appropriate victory sign, well at least he thought it was appropriate! Upon return to the paddock, the car was quickly checked over, and then it was my turn. But no, practice had just come to a halt for the local church service, more waiting and tension. However, in a way this proved of help as another RAC Sprint Championship pacemaker, Johnty Williamson, was also competing at the meeting with his ultra rapid Manpower Surtees Chevrolet and he very kindly offered to drive me around the circuit in his road car and give me the benefit of his considerable experience. Now whether this was really beneficial or not is still open to debate, for Johnty really is one of the characters of sprinting, with a particularly dry sense of humour. As we lined his road car up on the start line, which was exceptionally wide, the runway, which formed part of the opening stretch of the mile and a quarter circuit sprint, dipped out of view after a quarter of a mile, but according to Johnty, even in a powerful racing car, you went over the brow on full power. However, just after the brow there were some straw bales to narrow the course slightly, so one had to remember to keep to the left over the brow and down towards a fairly tight right-hand bend, which led through a left sweep to another tight right-hander. Johnty stopped here and pointed way across the grass towards a hedge, and with his usual wry grin pointed out the spot, way in the distance, where you would finish up if things went wrong. Very reassuring it was for a beginner. From the right-hander, a fairly wide and fast straight led back to a right-handed hairpin and the finish line. The competition runs would consist of two laps, so you had to get it right twice to be assured of a good time.

Thankfully by the time we returned to the paddock the church service was nearly completed, and so it was into the car and to the paddock exit. Motoring onto the course I was confronted by one brother-in-law complete with camera, determined not to let this opportunity of getting one over me pass. As I nosed onto the line what was it that Dave said, "4,000 revs and drop the clutch," Hmm, sounds a lot but let's try it — the light goes green and you are on your own now boy, dip the clutch and snick the gearlever into second gear, the car momentarily edges forward, but no problems, right then, gentle throttle, no not that much, as the rev counter flies to 5,000 revs per minute. Try again, gently, that's it 4,000 rpm. "Drop the clutch", the seat hits me in the small of the back and the car lurches forward, only to stutter as the revs drop too low, and we seem to creep away from the start. Suddenly the motor picks up and that brow is flying towards us, and without thinking I have already made two gear changes. Up to the brow, remember to keep left — there are straw bales on the right, just missed them, and already the first right-hander is coming towards me. Hard on the brakes, and the car slows as rapidly as it accelerates, and I crawl into the corner at the same time finding a lower gear. Gently through the left-hand sweep and the next right-hander, and again vicious acceleration down to the hairpin.

The course is dusty here, and despite what appeared to be very early braking, a front wheel locks up in a plume of blue smoke, but all is well and it is on to the second lap again with no dramas. Crossing the finish line for the second time it is kill the engine and cruise back into the paddock. Well at least, even if it was not fast, you kept it on the island, and there are still three more runs to come before the end of the day. Upon arrival in the paddock I am informed that the time was 102 seconds. Ten seconds behind Dave but that can be bettered. Getting out of the car I notice my right-hand is covered in blood, funny I thought, that should not be there, and suddenly realised that in changing gear I had ripped a finger on the bodywork. Next lesson, learn how to grip the gear lever properly.

After Dave's second run we have another go, this time taking the bull by the horns and deciding to use another 500 revs off the line. That is too much, as the rear of the car is enveloped in tyre smoke and it snakes its way off the line almost out of control. There is no option, back off the power and straighten the car before all hell lets loose. By this time I am over the hump and approaching the first bend, braking a little later this time it proves a struggle to find the right gear, but with a nasty crunching sound it goes in, and that even with a problem must have been better than before. This time keep the power on through the fast left-hander. Dave says it is easy flat out, and so it proves until you arrive at the next right-hander obviously travelling much faster than before, still we should make it, down a gear OK. The engine is still on full song and the next minute the scenery is revolving. What happened, surely I was not going that fast. I shoot onto the grass, funnily enough it was Johnty's bend but I shot off on the other side of the course. Suddenly it is realised that the throttle is still half open, despite no pressure on the pedal, but a quick stab releases it, having checked the gauges to make sure that all was still well. It is now time to turn the car around gently on the grass, looking back to make sure that another car is not coming, as the course caters for four cars at a time although they start singly. With red face, I rejoin the course, and think that I might as well complete the second lap and get a time, after all it is all good experience. Suitably subdued the second run is completed, and surprisingly the time is only seven seconds slower than the first effort even with the spin.

The lunch break sees Dave's mechanic Ian attending to the sticking throttle, and so hopefully the afternoon run will bring better luck. As the McLaren is being shared by two drivers, the organisers decide that I shall run first, right at the start of the official runs, to enable Dave to run in his normal class order. So it is the McLaren which opens the meeting, lining up with three other cars, including Alan Cox with his Cooper S who is making signs of outright terror as I draw alongside. Stop laughing at him, it is not that bad and get on with it. As the light again goes green, it is decided to use just under 4500 revs for the start, and as the clutch is dropped the sensation of acceleration is phenomenal. That must have been right, and the start is the best yet with the runway hurtling up to meet me. Already I am through onto the back straight. That is better, this must be an improvement, however, it never pays to speak too soon, and by leaving the braking a little late into the last bend at the end of the first lap the car suddenly snaps out of line, causing a minor panic. Put on some opposite lock, that is better for after a little wrist waving, it is again going in the prescribed direction. But not that well. That would account for it, I am in far too high a gear, having in the panic to sort out the impending moment, failed to make the appropriate gear change, but suddenly the car again picks up and starts to rocket towards the brow. It could still be a better run, when suddenly the power goes and the car starts to come to a halt.

Oh no, I hope I have not blown it up. Dipping the clutch and with arm outstretched, there is nothing for it but to coast into the paddock entrance and retire. As I make my way along the return road to the paddock my eye suddenly falls upon a switch in the down position that should not be there, it is supposed to be up. Try it up, drop the car into gear and release the clutch, and yes the engine bursts back into life. I must have knocked it off when I got into trouble on the last bend, well at least the car is OK and Dave can take his run. However, that was far from the end of the day's problems for on his first run Dave only managed a couple of hundred yards before the drive shaft broke at about one hundred miles an hour causing considerable damage to the suspension and certainly that was the end of the sport for the day.

All that remained was to take the transporter to the far side of the course and load up the broken McLaren. Whilst I decided, despite the disappointment of not being able to take another run and perhaps get somewhere near getting in a good time, to stay and watch the rest of the meeting, Dave's wife decided that perhaps it might be a good idea for him to turn his attentions to the wilderness at home, and so he set sail for home, at the end of a disappointing day. However, from my own point of view the experience of driving an ultra competitive racing car is one that I shall never forget, despite the disappointments, but this only goes to show the ups and downs that even a potential national champion can suffer, for although Dave's luck was out at the club event at

Wroughton, it certainly did not desert him the following year, for he went on to become the 1975 RAC National Sprint Champion, having virtually dominated the series in the car that I drove. Now we follow religiously the stars in the newspaper, for perhaps one day that forecast windfall will actually materialise and a similar car can be purchased. There is no doubt that to drive a full blooded single seater racing car is the ultimate motor sport sensation.

14 A trip to the top - a speed climb with Championship contender Chris Cramer

Having taken a look at a sprint course, at speed, from the cockpit of Dave Harris' McLaren, let us now turn our attentions to a hillclimb, which in direct contrast to our sprint venue, leaves no room whatsoever for error, being lined with trees, banks and stone walls, often only inches from the edge of the tarmac course. In the past few seasons, Stroud architect Chris Cramer has emerged from a highly successful period in Minis and sports racing cars as one of the top single seater racing car drivers, taking his two litre Brian Hart engined Grunhalle Lager March to many fastest times of the day awards in 1974 and 1975 and placing his name in the record books on several occasions before campaigning his 3.4 litre March in 1976. Wherever there is a championship hillclimb, Chris will be amongst the leading contenders for outright victory. Let us look at the sport through his eyes, enjoy it, and learn some of his secrets.

"Speed hillclimbing is probably the most exacting and concentrated form of motor sport, for everything hangs in the balance, as a driver and his car, working as one, strive to record a single really rapid climb. Twenty, thirty, or usually at the most, forty seconds separate your start from the moment when you flash over the finish line, cut your engine and wait to hear the time for that run, wondering if you have improved on your previous efforts, or even broken the class or outright hill record. Into the short space which such a climb takes, you will have condensed more problems and effort than the average driver achieves in twelve months motoring on the normal highway.

"Every speed hillclimb presents a driver with its own problems, each one different, needing a special application of skill and thought to overcome. Such is the challenge of an event that even two consecutive runs, on the same course, can provide different problems. Changes in the temperature can cause the entire characteristics of the track surface to alter, which will in turn unbalance the settings of the car, which are so important in the closely fought world of championship speed hillclimbing. In many other forms of motor sport you can assess your own chances of victory when you cross the finishing line, for you can see the opposition, either just creeping ahead of you, or perhaps looming large in your mirrors, with the chequered flag in sight. In complete contrast, the hillclimb driver has no visual check whatsoever on his performance during a run, for although there may be more than one car on the course during an event, they still start singly. It is just a battle, the driver and his car, against that invisible clock which unmercifully ticks away in the timekeeper's hut. The slightest lapse in concentration, the least hint of a slide in the wrong place, or even a momentary misfire of the engine will cost you those few vital hundredths, even thousandths of a second, that can mean the difference between success and failure.

"At the end of his first run, a driver cannot simply sit back, relax and wait for his next climb. To be competitive throughout the day, he must replay his last run in his own mind, attempting to plan the next climb, trying to work out where a little time can be made up on the next run. At first glance, it may seem almost impossible to improve upon the last run, but no driver has ever completed the totally perfect climb, and somewhere, somehow, it is always possible to improve, albeit sometimes by only a minute fraction of a second.

But that might just be enough to snatch victory from the other hard chasing, and equally experienced, championship contenders.

"To give you an idea of just what goes on during a championship hillclimb, it may be best to concentrate on one event in some detail.

"Imagine that you are paying your first visit to Bouley Bay, on the northern coast of the beautiful Channel Island of Jersey, whilst I set the scene for you, by describing those features which make this hill so different from all the other hillclimb courses in Great Britain. I have always enjoyed competing here, and indeed it was at Bouley Bay that I scored my third RAC Championship victory in July 1974. Bouley Bay is normally visited by the mainland competitors only once a year, and so there is inevitably a great deal of 'brushing up' to be done, as we refresh our memories of the problems which this hill presents. Inevitably each visit brings out new subleties, things which we have never noticed before, but which, if we can interpret them correctly, may conceivably explain just why we go so well on one part of the hill, and yet only a few yards further on, find the going so difficult. Although Bouley Bay is only a one thousand yard climb, (like many of the mainland hills), there are a number of factors which make it unique in the championship series. Possibly the most striking point of the course is the width of the road, which unlike most of the other hillclimb courses, is a two lane public highway, being specially closed for the hillclimb to take place. Being a two lane road (which incidentally is well used by holidaymakers, as it leads to a particularly attractive little bay), the road has a white line down the centre, and contains various cross cambers along its length. The considerable volume of holiday traffic which uses this road daily, leaves behind a fair amount of oil and rubber dust, on what otherwise appears to be an extremely good surface. This is very deceptive, for the grime from normal everyday traffic can make the course surprisingly slippery under competition conditions, especially if the weather turns sour, when rain can turn the entire hill into a skating rink.

"All of the corners on the Bouley Bay course are 'blind', and since there are no obvious landmarks, it is extremely difficult to establish positions on the course to use as exact indicators for the braking points, which are vital in producing a winning climb. The course contains three hairpin bends, as well as a tight 'S' bend, which follows the start, and winds its way around the local beach cafe. These bends demand that the basic quality of the car should be good traction, which is the ability to transfer its power onto the road with the maximum effect. The hairpins are connected by deceptively fast curves, often under the shadow of trees, which can produce further problems, as the sunlight finds its way through the breaks in the foliage, giving a peculiar patchy light effect at track level. The curves vary from the very tight Radio Hairpin bend, to the much faster *Les Platons.* The final hairpin, which is close to the finish line, appears to be the easiest of all, but has a very deceptive braking point which tempts the driver to 'go too deep' into the corner, only to find that he has 'overshot' the real apex and lost time. At championship level this certainly amounts to a wasted run.

"These problems can also be aggravated by a driver sensing that up to this point his run has gone well, and therefore he allows himself to relax the element of restraint which is of particular importance on this part of the course. A split second can see the undoing of some forty seconds worth of extremely hard work, concentration, and ten-tenths effort. Once the final hairpin has been successfully negotiated, the majority of the task is completed, for all that remains is the short straight to the finish line, which calls for hard acceleration and probably one further crisp and accurately executed gear change.

"After looking at the layout of the hill and refreshing our memories of the problems which this particular course presents, we can prepare to take our first run of the meeting. Firstly, we must carry out all the checks and preliminaries necessary with a single seater racing car. The Hart racing engine of my Grunhalle Lager March is started, and carefully warmed up, whilst at the same time the gauges are checked to ensure that all is well. The most vital gauges to watch are those indicating the oil and water temperatures, for to start with a cold engine will mean not only poor performance, but also the danger of an expensive mechanical disaster. It is also vital that the water temperature does not rise into the danger area at the other end of the scale.

"The car is then brought to the start line, with one eye still watching the gauges, and the other one waiting for the green light which flashes on when the course is clear, indicating that I can start as soon as I am ready. Suddenly the light turns green. A quick glance at the gauges show normal readings as I engage first gear. The engine revs are built up, and the clutch released, causing deliberate wheelspin which turns to traction as the tyres grip the tarmac, and this produces fierce acceleration. A quick change into second gear is made as I move over to the right of the road, lining the car up for the tricky 'S' bend. Now brake hard, change down to first gear, and at virtually the same time lock the car into the left-hand part of the 'S' bend, taking advantage of the road camber. Just clip the solid stone wall on a late apex, then switch across the centre of the road again, using the road camber

The Grunhalle Lager March of
Chris Cramer finding the right
line at Radio Corner, Bouley Bay

David Franklin demonstrates the
art of early application of power
as he exits one of the tighter bends
on the Wroughton sprint course
with his March 742 BMW

to full advantage. Coming through the right-hand part of the bend on a late apex, allows me to get the power in early and progressively, whilst checking a tail slide as the car momentarily tries to take control. It is then hard on the power, with the car accelerating rapidly. Up through two gears, and I am already into the next bend, which is the fastest on the course, requiring only a dab on the brakes, whilst keeping the car to the left-hand side of the road. Turning into this bend late I note that as I apex the corner, the car, now travelling very quickly indeed, starts to feel 'very light', a sensation like hitting black ice, causing it to 'float' across the road. Correct application of power, whilst at the same time continuing to hold a controlled slide, takes me from this point into the following left-hand curve. Maintaining hard acceleration, a wall flashes into sight ahead, requiring hard braking, and a change down into second gear, whilst at the same time keeping the car out to the right as I approach this open hairpin. Turning in late, the close line allows me to take a late apex, and make the best use once again of the road cambers, saving a few vital hundredths of a second as I do so.

"A fast exit out of this hairpin bend, on a correct line, is absolutely vital, as I can then hold a controlled power slide through the following right and left curve, whilst at the same time changing up into third gear. The

Warm tyres are essential for a rapid start. Here, Tony Griffiths warms up his rear tyres of the Brabham BT33 prior to a run at Doune

Typical of many of the single seater cars which compete in both hillclimbs and sprints is the Ford Twin Cam engined Brabham BT21B of Basil Thomas. He is another man to graduate to single seater cars having served his apprenticeship in a Mini

road really is 'on the move' around here, and the best use of the road camber is essential for a truly fast passage through this section. I can now allow the car to drift towards the bank at the Marshal's Post, marking the very tricky left curve approaching the incredibly tight right-hand hairpin known as Radio Corner, which is lined with all sorts of hazards. Having braked, and changed into first gear, I go into this bend relatively slowly, taking a late apex, and at the same time trying to avoid the projecting rocks on the inside of the bend, for these have claimed the rear wheels of many competitors in the past. It is now essential to control the power slide out of this corner, in order to avoid the sheer rock face on the outside of the bend. Maintaining hard, but controlled acceleration, to avoid 'tail end snake', which can cost vital time, I snatch third gear for the short, slightly right-hand curving climb up to the last hairpin. Here I have to brake seemingly early, change down through the gearbox, with the car weaving about under the heavy deceleration, and yet again aim for a late apex. At this point, I can turn on the power, change up to second gear as the tail slides out, and allow the car to drift across to the outside of the road, as I accelerate over the finish line.

"As soon as the car has crossed the line, the engine is cut, and with any luck I can just catch the time for my climb as it comes over the public address system. What was it? How does it compare with the times set by the other competitors? As with most good hillclimbs there is virtually no way of telling, and often what appeared from the cockpit to be a good run, results in a slightly disappointing time, whilst a record breaking run can come as a complete surprise, but then, that is the fascination of hillclimbing."

Although it has taken several minutes to enjoy a climb at Bouley Bay with Chris, in reality this is far from the case, for all the twists and turns, endless gear changes, and applications of the brakes are condensed into just a few seconds on the road. Incredibly, despite the numerous problems which the one thousand yard course poses, Chris has completed the climb in just 42.80 seconds with the two litre March — an average speed of nearly fifty miles an hour from a standing start, which as you have seen includes three vicious hairpin bends. You will have gathered by now, that vital fractions of a second can easily be lost at Bouley Bay, and it is this which surely makes it one of the great hillclimbs, where speed, roadholding and driving skill all contribute to the result.

The 1975 RAC Championship event at Bouley Bay must rate as one of the best events in recent years, the closeness of the competition being ably demonstrated by Chris, with the 2.2 litre Grunhalle Lager March, and the 5 litre Chevrolet powered Fenny Marine GM1 of Roy Lane. Their battle in the Top Ten Championship run-off will long be remembered, with Roy taking the lead on the first run at 43.00 seconds, only to see Chris on his second climb move into the lead by the smallest of margins with a time of 42.99 seconds. Everything turned again on the very last run of the day, when Roy finally managed to take the award, slipping ahead of Chris by just two one hundredths of a second. Three runs by two drivers, in two very different cars, over a one thousand yard course, with only three one hundredths of a second between them. That, however, is typical of the competitiveness of the sport, and only goes to prove the point made by Chris, that even the smallest fraction of a second can make all the difference between winning and losing.

Prolific record breaker Alister Douglas Osborn really fighting to keep his Motosail (Jersey) Pilbeam R22 DFV on the Island at Bouley Bay

15 The mechanics

With the sport of hillclimbing and sprinting developing, as it has over the last few years, into a highly competitive and sophisticated form of motor racing, it is not surprising to see the competing machinery for this unique sport turning into specialised, and sometimes highly strung cars. A few years ago, even amongst the racing car classes, it was customary to arrive at a meeting with the car, unload it, compete in the event, and then reload it onto the trailer, and head for home. Barring a breakdown or engine problems, it was quite usual for even a championship contender to go through the day without working on his steed. With the advances which have come about in the last few years, as the competitiveness of the sport has increased beyond all bounds, a new role for the driver has arrived, that of mechanic, for as we have already seen, the track conditions, and in fact the atmosphere, can change between runs. This can call for the car to be drastically reset in many respects, if the next climb is to be competitive.

Perhaps the biggest development over the years, has come in the field of tyres. Whereas in the olden days, one set of tyres would suffice for a competition car, no matter what the track or weather conditions, this is no longer the case. A selection of tyres is now available, each type suitable for a certain kind of condition, and often virtually lethal if used at the wrong time. For the dry course, the championship contenders will almost always select the slick tyre, a tyre which features no tread whatsoever, and this can often provide a great advantage over the grooved version. Should the course be wet, then the slick will prove totally useless and extremely dangerous, for with no tread and hence channelling, the water beneath the tyre cannot escape, causing the car to aquaplane and rapidly go out of control. It is in conditions like this that the grooved wet weather tyre is essential, whilst many drivers also carry an intermediate group tyre for use when the course is neither dry or streaming wet. In addition to these various types of tyre, there are many combinations of rubber mix, which can also drastically affect the handling of the car. The driver must decide which of these many options is the correct one for each particular run, a difficult task, especially as an error in the choice will often result in a most uncompetitive time.

With the modern day racing car, it is also possible to change the actual ratios in the gearbox between runs, without too much difficulty. This is yet another decision which faces the driver, for often he will feel that at a particular point on the course the car is perhaps not accelerating as well as it could do, or is perhaps over-revving. This can be rectified by a change of the gear ratios, but again the margins are fine. Often just one slight change can produce an improvement by a substantial margin, whilst on the other hand a slight mistake in the choice of gearing can cost a tremendous amount of time. Often you will see drivers in the paddock changing gears between runs, in an attempt to find those few vital fractions of a second, or to combat the track conditions which may be rapidly changing.

The modern single seater hillclimb and sprint car now often exceeds one hundred miles an hour during the course of a speed event. The handling of the car must therefore be as near to perfection as can be possibly achieved. All the competitive racing cars feature adjustable suspension, and often a minute change to the settings can drastically improve matters. With the advent of wings and spoilers, which help to keep the car stable through the faster reaches of the course, by acting similarly to an aircraft wing but in reverse, this again brings further problems. The suspension and the wing and spoiler angles can be adjusted, whilst some drivers even carry different nose cones for the car, as this can again affect the handling. To arrive at the near perfect setting, with so many variables, requires a tremendous aptitude for the feeling of the motor car during a run and surprisingly, although the majority of the championship hillclimb and sprint competitors are not even involved in the motor trade, they manage to find the infinite line between near perfection and disaster. There are many other variables to be taken into account, and many slight modifications to be equated, before a car is totally suited to a particular venue. Really the only way to appreciate the tremendous amount of thought and work which goes into making a competitive run on a hillclimb or sprint is to visit the paddock during a meeting, watch the drivers, often with the help of a part time mechanic, fettling their cars in preparation for their next run. Hillclimbing and sprinting could almost be classed as a science, and certainly if you do visit the paddock, I am sure you will find it hard to disagree.

Of course, although the event can see a certain amount of fettling in an effort to make the car one hundred per cent efficient on the day, the main bulk of the preparation work will take place, usually at the competitor's own home, during the week. There are few drivers who can afford to employ a full time mechanic to look after the car, and almost without exception, the majority of the maintenance work will be carried out by the competitor himself, during the weekday evenings. This really can be a time-consuming job, often taking virtually all the available time between meetings. The standard of preparation of hillclimb and sprint machinery has, in the past few years, improved beyond all recognition, a tremendous feat, especially when one considers that almost without exception, the competitors have extremely limited facilities. The life of a hillclimb and sprint car is a rigorous one, with the transmission and engine in particular taking a tremendous pounding, and there are always little problems facing the competitor in the week. These must be solved before the next weekend, and usually are, whether it be an engine re-build, a gearbox repair, or simply attention to the bodywork which might have been damaged by an off-course excursion. Certainly hillclimbing and sprinting can be rated as a full time hobby, for once the event is completed, the planning and fettling for the next meeting begins, and this can be a mighty task, especially if the weekend has been marred with an abnormal problem. The incidence of non-starters at most meetings, proves the dedication of the average competitor, for only a major disaster will prevent him, or her, from taking their place on the start line the following weekend.

With the current V8 Chevrolet engines producing some 500 brake horse power, the drive shafts to the wheels have to be extremely strong

The office

Most modern racing cars are fitted with an 'air box' to duct the air to the carburettors or fuel injection system when at speed

Although built on a shoestring, the 1300cc turbocharged March driven by Andy Smith and Rob Oldaker proved a surprise to many of the 1600cc powered cars

Nose cones can often transform the handling of a car, notice two different fronts to the Brabham BT35X of Malcolm Dungworth

The setting of the rear wing on a racing car can be all important and often minor adjustments are made between runs to improve the performance of the car

Chris Cramer demonstrates the meaning of the word understeer as he tries to pull the front of the March around the tight Wis Corner at Wiscombe Park

Correct tyre pressure are an essential in the competitive speed sports world and are usually checked after every run, no matter how short

Dust can often provide a problem to hillclimbers and sprinters, along with the cement dust which is put on any oil which may be dropped on the track. Here Ken MacMaster shows how large the problem can be as the dust and cement pour off the front wheels

16 Records through the years -is it the cars or the drivers

Although it is scarcely three quarters of a century since the advent of the motor car, and its first use in an officially organised hillclimb at Shelsley Walsh, the amount of development which has taken place in that comparatively short time has been phenomenal. Let us drop in on that first ever Shelsley event, where forty one of those new fangled machines had gathered to do battle over the then dirt based course, of one thousand yards in length. As with any new development, there were numerous teething troubles, at least five cars failing to make the top of the hill at all, let alone climb it at a respectable speed, whilst others required nearly five minutes to make the ascent! However, perhaps the most surprising element of that first ever hillclimb, was the closeness of the competition, for eventually the fastest time of the day fell to E. Instone with a run of 77.6 seconds, in his 35 horse power Daimler. But even in those dark and early days of the sport he only achieved victory by the narrow margin of six tenths of a second, from the similar car of A. Birtwistle.

In the early days, just one meeting a year was held at Shelsley, but already the quest for speed was on, and although the White Steam Car of F. Coleman, who won the next event, failed to better the previous years' time set by Instone, 1907 saw a return to close competition, with the Berliet of J. Hutton, and the Talbot of T. Bowen tying for the honour of the fastest time of the day. In the process they took over ten seconds off the outright hill record. This trend of improvement carried on, at only slightly abated pace, until by 1924 the Beardmore of Cyril Paul was knocking on the door of a sub fifty second run. He set a new best mark for the hill of 50.6 seconds.

The sport was beginning to attract some of the fastest circuit racing cars which both Great Britain and the Continent could muster. Already by this time Raymond Mays, who was to become a legend at Shelsley, had made his mark, for the year before Paul's record, he too put his name in the record books when driving his Bugatti, he shared fastest time of the day with the Vauxhall of M. Park. Although the 1925 event was won by the Sunbeam of no less a person than Sir Henry Seagrave, it was not until the next year that the fifty second barrier was beaten, when the incredible Basil Davenport stormed to victory at 48.8 seconds. He repeated this victory on two further consecutive occasions, so that by the end of 1928 the Shelsley record had already been reduced from 77.6 seconds to 46.2 seconds. The trend continued with the Vauxhall Villiers of Raymond Mays maintaining, by now the almost traditional move, of winning the yearly meeting with a new hill record. He took the event in 1929 at 45.6 seconds, but the year that will be long remembered in the history of Shelsley, and indeed British hillclimbing, is 1930, for that saw the appearance of Hans Stuck in the incredible works entered Austro Daimler. He lived up to expectations, by taking two point eight seconds off the record, leaving it at 42.8 seconds.

By now, of course, the surface at Shelsley had been much improved from the original days, and this certainly contributed in part to the improvement in times. The meeting which in the 1930s, attracted International drivers, also served to bring forth the faster racing cars of the period, as opposed to the road cars which were used in the earlier days. It was in 1932 that Shelsley, which attracted thousands of spectators, began to stage two meetings a year, but despite the appearance of the fastest cars and drivers of the time, Hans Stuck's record remained intact until 1933. It was the fabulous Maserati of Whitney Straight which demolished it, reducing it to 41.2 seconds. At the June meeting the following year it was further reduced to 40.0 seconds. The big question on everyone's lips was "Who would break 40 seconds for the first time?" Well the answer came in May 1935, for Raymond Mays and the ERA fittingly became the first combination to beat the barrier, fittingly, as Mays has won considerably more Shelsley Walsh events than any other driver in the history of the venue. It was Mays who dominated the next four meetings with his all conquering ERA, but despite equalling his record on one occasion, it remained otherwise unchallenged until the June of 1937, when with the timing equipment for the first time recording to one hundredth of a second, he wrestled his car to the top in 39.09 seconds. But his record was short lived, as in September of the same year, the Frazer Nash of A. F. P. Fane had brought it into the 38 second range. Mays was quick to react, snatching it back just two meetings later, and in June 1939, the last meeting before the cessation of events at Shelsley due to the war, he really made his mark with a great effort of 37.37 seconds.

Upon resumption of activities at Shelsley in 1946, Mays continued virtually to dominate the proceedings, but despite a string of winning runs, he never quite managed to equal his last pre-war time. It was not until the June of 1949, that this long standing record tumbled, and then by only two hundredths of a second, as the fearsome Freikaiserwagen of Joe Fry recorded 37.35 seconds. Then came a sensation, for in the September, ace motorcyclist George Brown really shook everyone, by taking the outright hill record with a fantastic climb of 37.13 seconds on his 1000cc HRD. Despite the attentions of such up and coming drivers as Ken Wharton, with his supercharged Cooper, who reduced Fry's car record to 37.27 seconds, the outright record still remained with Brown. However the supercharged Cooper of Wharton was really the car to beat in the early 1950s, and in September 1951 he regained the record for the car brigade, with a storming climb of 36.62 seconds. In June 1953 he trimmed it by a further two hundredths of a second. However for 1954 Wharton returned to the ERA camp, and again proved immediately successful making a climb of 35.80 seconds in the August, and this record really did prove a fine one.

It was not until the June of 1958 that Tony Marsh, the man who has won the RAC Hillclimb Championship more times than any other driver, came onto the scene with a bang, trimming the record by a fifth of a second with his Cooper. Welshman David Boshier-Jones then took over with his JAP powered Cooper, and again the record was broken, this time in August 1959, as Boshier-Jones climbed the hill 0.13 seconds quicker than anyone before. This record lasted into the early 1960s, which saw the advent of the modern rear engined single seater racing car onto the hill, and in August 1961, Tony Marsh with his magnificent BRM swept almost serenely up the hill in just 34.41 seconds. By 1963 he had even reduced this by just under another second to 33.54 seconds. The honour of holding the next record fell to the supercharged Lotus of Peter Boshier-Jones, the brother of former record holder David, who put his name in the record books in 33.35 seconds, but it was not long before that man Marsh was at it again, and the next year, with his home constructed Marsh Special, he managed 32.94 seconds. This record stood for three meetings until Marsh, with his by then American V8 engined car, really set everyone talking with a tremendous improvement to 31.23 seconds, but even this record lasted only until the next meeting. By this time the American engined cars were stamping their mark well and truly on the hillclimb scene, and Bryan Eccles, with his Buick powered Brabham, reduced Marsh's mark by 0.4 seconds.

You will remember that in the early days of Shelsley a tie for the fastest time of the day and a new record was achieved, when timing to one tenth of a second. This was not destined to happen again, at least not quite, but in August 1969 Martin Brain set yet another new record at 30.72 seconds, a time which was equalled by the McLaren of Sir Nicholas Williamson the following June. Again the record was to be short lived, as onto the scene came a tremendous character, by the name of David Hepworth, with a four wheel drive Brabham based, home built car, and at the next meeting the record was standing to his credit at just 30.49 seconds, and excitement mounted, as that magic sub half-minute climb, which everybody knew must be possible was awaited. Well, it was not a long wait, for Hepworth having set his first Shelsley record in August 1970, returned the following June, and there it was 29.92 seconds. As if to prove the point, just two months later, he further improved to 29.64 seconds. However in August 1972, a gentleman by the name of Mike MacDowel, a former works circuit racing driver for the Cooper team, was more than making his own mark on the hillclimb scene, and he began a run of success at Shelsley. He was destined to win five meetings in a row with his Repco V8 powered Brabham BT36X, his first win setting a new record at 29.29 seconds, just incredible everyone thought, but just one meeting later he was at it again with a sub twenty nine second run, 28.82 seconds. Even this was not the end for just two months later he had returned an almost unbelievable 28.21 second run. Despite taking two more victories at Shelsley before temporarily retiring from single seater hillclimbing, not even Mike could quite come to terms

Sprint exponent Johnty
Williamson relives the historic
days of Shelsley Walsh by giving
his ERA a run up the hill during
a cavalcade

The Lightweight Special, one of the
firm favourites at hillclimbs during
past years, and still going strong

with that superb record which looked like standing for many a long year.

However in 1975 Roy Lane had other ideas, and at the height of a record breaking season, which was to net him the RAC Hillclimb Championship with a maximum points score, the first time that this feat had been achieved in the history of the series, Lane came to Shelsley with his virtually all conquering Fenny Marine GM1 Chevrolet. His second practice run exactly equalled MacDowels's record, and the paddock was buzzing, perhaps after all it was just beatable. A couple of hours later the whole of Shelsley was momentarily stunned as Lane's third practice time was announced, not only had he beaten MacDowel's record but had just slipped into the 27 second bracket. What a climb, but practice does not count, he had to repeat it in the event for it to stand as a record. Lane dominated the proceedings but despite a mammoth effort could not quite repeat a 27 second run, although he well and truly took MacDowel's record leaving it at 28.03 seconds and proved that a 27 second run was possible.

Well, as you can imagine, it was not long before the record was indeed reduced to below the twenty eight second mark, but such is the pace of modern day hillclimbing that even the real hillclimb pundits were amazed by the performance of one man in particular. That man was Alister Douglas Osborn, who really made Shelsley Walsh his hill in 1976, with his Formula One engined Pilbeam DFV. Alister's climbs of the hill in 1976 just had to be seen to be believed, for his enthusiastic performances on the fast and dangerous slopes, brought gasps of disbelief, from even the most ardent followers of the sport. The black projectile, on many climbs at Shelsley

Typical of the many 'Shelsley Specials' over the years, the motorcycle engined Djinn still remains extremely fleet of foot especially in a straight line sprint

One of the most remarkable cars ever seen at Shelsley Walsh, the GN Spider of Basil Davenport, the hill record holder many years ago

during the year, seemed beyond the point of no return, as it twitched and snaked its way up the hill at speeds exceeding one hundred and twenty miles an hour, but although it might have looked just a little too 'hairy' for comfort, Alister knew precisely the limits to which he could push the car, and not only reduced the record to the low 27 second mark, but really showed that within a few meetings, the record book will have to be re-written into the 26 second range, with an incredible practice run at 27.12 seconds.

So in the short space of seventy years the record at Shelsley has been reduced from 77.6 seconds to just over 27 seconds, with further improvement already seemingly possible. Where will it end, what is the ultimate? Who knows, it is probable that man's reflexes will one day prove to be the deciding factor, for throughout the history of hillclimbing, constant development and the desire to climb a course a little faster each time, has seen monumental developments in competition cars. Although this progress can never now advance as dramatically as in the past, it will continue, to provide faster and better racing cars. Already a driver is working at absolute capacity to keep the modern day racing car on the straight and narrow. It is an enthralling battle, which man is constantly winning, as he proves by setting new records. It will continue to improve for many years, and as it does we can only speculate at where that ultimate may be. It would have been interesting to ask our friend, Instone, who set the first record at Shelsley in 1905, where he thought the ultimate lay at that time. It must be an even bet, that even he could not have forseen 27 second runs in 1976, if the progress continues at such a rate, by 2050 we could expect, by that yardstick, 10 second runs. Ridiculous is it not, or is it? Who knows?

17 Why do they do it? ~ the personalities

As we have seen this far, literally thousands of everyday people are involved in the sport of hillclimbing and sprinting, at a multitude of events throughout Great Britain. There really remains one puzzling problem, why do they do it? What exactly is the fascination of this sport, which in its own way is unique to Great Britain? The answer to that question is rather like the mountaineers' reply when asked, "Why do you climb these dangerous peaks," the answer almost inevitably being, "Because they're there," in itself a roundabout way of saying "I don't really know." There must, however, be many reasons why the amateur hillclimber and sprint driver weekly risks his life, in what can be an exceedingly dangerous sport. If things go wrong. The standard reply from most competitors, is that they go racing each weekend purely because they enjoy it. However, there are other factors, perhaps one being that it gives the competitor a chance of competing in a modern ultra competitive machine, whilst at the same time enjoying the fun and social atmosphere of an event, that perhaps circuit races do not provide. The sport of hillclimbing and sprinting, as we have reiterated many times, is a battle between a team, the driver and his car, and that unceasing enemy, time, an enemy that cannot be totally defeated, but an opponent that provides weekly, a new challenge.

The average hillclimber and sprinter invariably will be the sort of person that is never totally satisfied with the performance of any task that he or she might attempt, the sort of person that is always striving to improve, no matter what. This is proved many times weekly, for it is usually very few, if any, of the competitors who will go home and actually admit that they could not have bettered their time somewhere along the line. It perhaps all boils down to the fact that each competitor aims to be the first driver to record the ultimate run, a one hundred per cent perfect ascent. Not only are the events a battle between the car, driver, and the clock, but also between other competitors in the class, and this tends to breed a unique and friendly atmosphere. Often whilst husbands battle furiously on the track, the wives congregate together, to discuss various subjects in complete harmony. This is just a part, there are many more aspects, but once again they are so difficult to define. In a nutshell the sport is what it is because " . . . . ", well when you have seen an event and fallen for its special charisma, perhaps you may be able to say just why you have been hooked. Perhaps the real answer is that it is like a drug, fortunately a very pleasant one with no nasty side effects.

As you will have gathered by now, many of the hundreds of competitors are extremely successful in both hillclimbing and sprinting. There are of course many more drivers, who will regularly compete in events, knowing that their chances of success are slim, but nevertheless thoroughly enjoying their participation in the sport. To list even the successful drivers would need a separate book, at least as large as this one. I have selected below some of the very top drivers in British hillclimbing and sprinting, some already at the top of the tree in their chosen sport, others who are knocking on the door, and are certainly worth watching during the next few seasons.

Roy Lane

Roy Lane must be rated as one of the all time greats in hillclimbing, for not only does he always prove extremely competitive on the track, he also brings to the sport his own natural infectious brand of fun. These include such athletic activities as cycle races and cricket matches, whilst any post-event get together is certainly not complete without Roy, and his dedicated family, who really do prove the point that hillclimbing is for fun, win or lose. Roy originally started his successful sporting career, not with powered wheels, but in the saddle of a racing cycle, scoring many prestigious wins, and taking several records. He then progressed to circuit racing, from the very outset of his motor sporting career, building and maintaining his cars at home in Warwick. However, following a rather nasty accident at Silverstone, Roy decided that with a wife and family, circuit racing was not for him, and so ten years ago took to hillclimbing. Roy's hillclimb career is by no means a fairy tale, for his whole championship effort, throughout the years, has always been executed on an extremely limited budget. The majority of the mechanical work on the cars is carried out by Roy himself in the evenings, with dedicated assistance from wife Betty and children Anthony and Julie, and even to this day the light in the Lane garage can often be seen burning well beyond midnight.

Upon taking up hillclimbing in the mid 1960s, Roy did not make an immediate impression on the scene, but he persevered and gradually success came. Still, to this day, his eyes light up when he recalls the scoring of his first ever National championship point at Wiscombe Park, at that time a real stepping stone in the battle to tackle the pacemakers in the sport. As the years progressed, so did Roy's prowess, and in the late 1960s he really was becoming one of the men to watch on the hillclimb scene, and in fact finished in second spot in the RAC Championship. However, Roy, like any dedicated enthusiast, was not happy to accept even a second place, and still strove towards that championship win. The going was tough, but he refused to accept defeat, finishing in fourth place in both 1972 and 1973. The next season saw Mike MacDowel with his Brabham Repco, the 1973 champion, almost dominating the series, but Roy pressed him every inch of the way, and finished in second place overall at the end of the season.

Even at that point, no one realised just what a difficult man to beat Roy would be in 1975. Although the year began with a slight disappointment, at not winning the first round of the championship at Loton Park, it was not long before Roy and the Fenny Marine GM1 Chevrolet, were in full cry on the hills of Great Britain. From May onwards Roy really stamped his mark on the proceedings, and went from strength to strength, finally finishing the year with no less than eleven championship wins, winning that long strived for championship.

The maestro himself, Roy Lane, rounds the difficult Radio Corner at Bouley Bay with the Fenny Marine GM1 Chevrolet which took him to two hillclimb championships

Champion Year: Roy Lane complete with Fenny Marine GM1 and family having won the 1975 RAC Hillclimb Championship with a maximum points score

Fittingly for a man who had put so much effort into the sport, he achieved a maximum points score, the first time in the twenty five year history of the series that a perfect score had been made. Roy's first championship win was certainly a popular one, proving the point that with total dedication, and a tremendous amount of time and effort, an average working man can succeed in championship hillclimbing. Roy further underlined this point in 1976, for despite, in direct contrast to the previous year, coming under tremendous pressure in the championship chase, he remained unruffled and just held at bay the determined young driver, Alister Douglas Osborn, to take his second championship. It has been a terrific effort from not only Roy, but the whole family, which has taken him to the top in hillclimbing, but even with his ambition now twice achieved, Roy still plans to carry on in the sport, a sport that would definitely be poorer without his own special brand of humour. It is almost certain that the whole of the Lane family would be at a loss, if they could not, from week to week during the summer, take part in hillclimbs. Obviously they thoroughly enjoy the events, a fact that is very apparent if you are close to them during a meeting, even when things do not go well. Even a double champion has his share of problems. Perhaps for the whole of the Lane family, like so many others, hillclimbing has become, and always will be, an integral and vital part of their way of life.

Alister Douglas Osborn

A few seasons ago, Alister Douglas Osborn was almost an also-ran in the sports racing car class, with his elderly Mallock U2. However, upon purchasing a newer model of the same marque, he immediately began to show his paces. He soon became one of the men to beat in that particular class, and such was his success rate that he only just failed to pip Alex Brown for the title of RAC Leaders Hillclimb Champion. Following his excellent showing in the sports racing car class, it was almost certain to onlookers that here was a man to watch when he graduated to single seater racing cars. His followers were not disappointed, for in his first season of championship single seater hillclimbing with a Brabham BT38, he quickly showed his potential, taking an excellent fifth place overall in the series at his first attempt. For 1975 the Brabham was extensively modified by Mike Pilbeam, the man responsible for the BRM Formula One Grand Prix car, and with the drastically modified car now renamed the Pilbeam, Alister was set to really make an impression on the championship scene.

His start to the season was meteoric, for he really set his seal on the first RAC Championship event, the round at Loton Park, by staggering everyone with a fine outright win. However, at Prescott the next weekend he unfortunately lost control of the car at the top of the hill and damaged it quite badly. The car was rapidly repaired, and although Alister during the course of the year failed to repeat his Loton Park win, he proved

In 1975 Alister Douglas Osborn really made a mark on the hillclimb scene by taking his Pilbeam R15 BDG to third place overall in the RAC Hillclimb Championship

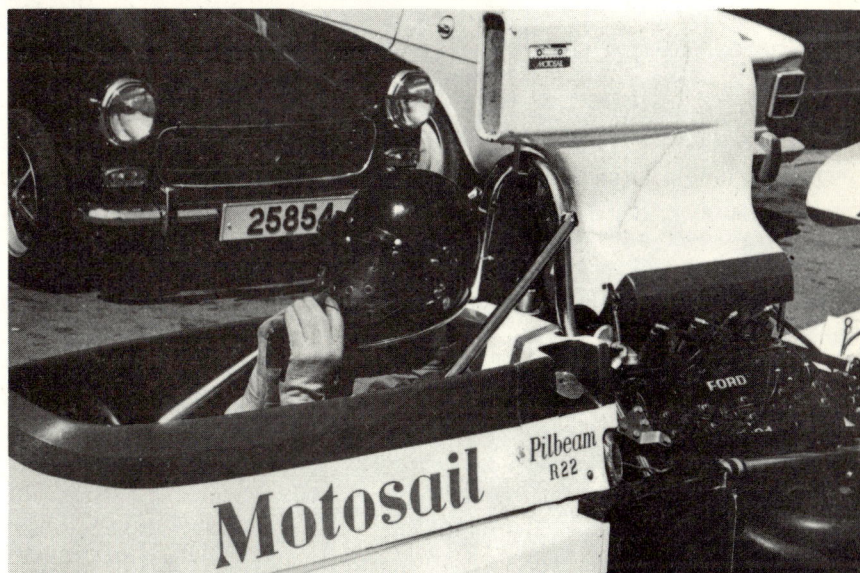

Let us pray! Alister Douglas Osborn prepares for another run

extremely rapid and consistent, often providing Chris Cramer with a real problem, although unable to quite challenge Roy Lane who really dominated the season. The result of consistent places throughout the year was an improvement to third place overall in the series, behind Lane and Cramer, but the best was still to come. For 1976 the car was returned to Mike Pilbeam, again drastically modified, and fitted with the Formula One DFV engine. This proved an enormous success, for Alister really arrived on the 1976 championship scene in a big way. He again started the year well with a win at Loton Park, but missed the first Prescott round to attend a wedding, a long standing promise to a friend, and possibly a very costly one. Alister really motored like never before, and constantly pressurised reigning champion Roy Lane, these two battling throughout the year. When on form Alister really was the man to beat, but he occasionally, as in the Channel Islands, seemed unable to quite get his runs together. However, by the end of the year, despite a bad dog bite on his hand which caused him great problems at the second Prescott round, he had won no less than six of the vital RAC Championship rounds, more than anyone else. Although he equalled Roy Lane's championship score, he was destined to take second place, on the tie-break rule, the same ruling which had cost him the Leaders Hillclimb Championship a few years earlier. However, despite by the smallest margins failing to take the RAC series, his performances with the Pilbeam, especially at Shelsley Walsh, where he consistently reduced the hill record as the season progressed, will be long remembered. He also excelled at other hills, taking amongst others the outright records at Doune and Wiscombe Park, clinching the FTD Awards championship within the Guyson/BARC series. Certainly the real man to watch in the future, Alister Douglas Osborn is, with the Motosail (Jersey) Ltd Pilbeam R22 DFV, possibly the hottest favourite for the RAC title for many years.

Chris Cramer

Possibly the most popular car amongst the clubmen for hillclimbing and sprinting, is the Mini Cooper S, and certainly, many star hillclimb names have emerged from the ranks of the saloon car drivers. One such person is Chris Cramer, the Stroud architect, and the driver of the Grunhalle Lager March. Chris originally began his motor sporting career behind the wheel of a go-kart, but upon making the transition to the world of hillclimbing, decided to start in the saloon car class, with a Mini Cooper S. Almost from the word go, he made his mark on the sport, virtually dominating his own particular class. Such was his prowess in the Cooper S, that many of his saloon car records still stand to this day. His next venture proved the only minor disaster of his otherwise extremely successful hillclimb career, for the Terrapin sports racing car which he then acquired, did not really prove itself. However, once he reverted to a BMC power unit in a Mallock U2, Chris was again on his way, dominating his particular class, and sweeping to a fine overall victory in the RAC Leaders Hillclimb Championship, the second time he had in fact taken that particular National title, having won it two years earlier in the Mini. 1973 saw Chris making his single seater racing car debut in hillclimbs with a March 74B, powered by a Hart engine, and sponsored by Grunhalle Lager. He quickly came to grips with this outright racing car, taking a fine fifth place overall in the RAC Hillclimb Championship at only his first attempt. The next year, with basically the same car, was an even bigger success story, for Chris progressed to third place overall in the championship series, in the process taking the outright course record at Bouley Bay, appropriately the Jersey hill adjacent to his sponsor. In many respects, 1975 must have been a slight disappointment for Chris, for although he retained the same car, and bettered his previous performances at most of the venues, he was facing a dramatically on-form Roy Lane. As always he persevered and despite a big challenge from Alister Douglas Osborn, managed to yet again better his overall championship placing, taking the runner-up spot to the Warwick driver.

Having finished in second place in the championship in 1975, Chris replaced the then 2.2 litre March 74B, with a dramatically new car. This car really excited everyone on the hillclimb scene for it saw the advent onto the hills of the Ford V6 engine which had proved to be successful in circuit racing. As with his earlier single seater, Chris used a March chassis, this time a brand new 76A, and as before the car was attractively presented in the colours of Grunhalle Lager. Obviously instant success could not be expected with the brand new car, but as with all his cars in the past, Chris applied himself with an almost clinical dedication to the task of turning it into a winner. In fact by May he was really coming into his own, winning the Barbon Manor round of the RAC Hillclimb Championship, albeit only on aggregate times from Roy Lane. Despite teething problems, Chris finished a well deserved third overall in the RAC Championship. This was indeed a fine effort in his first year with the new car. Chris really is a perfectionist, never totally satisfied with either his own performance, or the car's. He is constantly seeking new, and improved methods of producing that extra fraction of a second, which is the difference between success and defeat. His thoroughly professional attitude towards the sport of hillclimbing has already been rewarded with more than considerable success, and there are few people within the sport who would disagree with the statement that there is more to come.

Chris Cramer excited everyone in the hillclimb world in 1976, by appearing with a March 76A fitted with a 3.4 litre Ford based V6 engine and painted, of course, in the colour of his sponsor, Grunhalle Lager

Chris Cramer pondering on his next run

David Franklin

The success story of David Franklin, especially in the West Country, is now almost a legend amongst hillclimbers and sprinters. From his early beginnings with a Hillman Imp, in which he contested the local autocross events, David has developed into one of the country's fastest single seater racing car drivers. David quickly continued his record of success from the autocross fields. Like Chris Cramer, he was extremely successful in the saloon car class, proving a prolific winner, and setting many class records. His first venue into the single seater racing car class, saw him with a Hillman Imp powered Vixen, renamed the Huntsman Vixen, in deference to his business, Huntsman Garage near Bristol. David's smooth driving style soon made this diminutive, and well handling car, the one to beat in the up to 1100cc racing car class, and still to this day he holds class records set as long ago as 1973.

The natural progression was into the up to 1600cc racing car class, and so David purchased the ex Dempster Developments, Mike Wild, Ensign, for 1974. As with all his cars, the preparation to an exceedingly high standard, was undertaken by David, and his mechanics at the garage, naturally outside normal working hours. Just as with the Vixen, David excelled, and in only his first season with the car quickly showed that his earlier indicated potential was rapidly maturing. However, it is the 1975 season which David will probably remember longer than any other, for despite his comparative lack of power from the Holbay engine, he really shocked many of the top championship contenders. Although he did not compete in all the rounds of the RAC Hillclimb Championship,

Possibly the most successful car in 1975, the Huntsman Ensign of David Franklin, the Guyson/BARC Hillclimb Champion, sprint championship runner up and sixth in the RAC Hillclimb Championship rounds The Ashes at Gurston Down

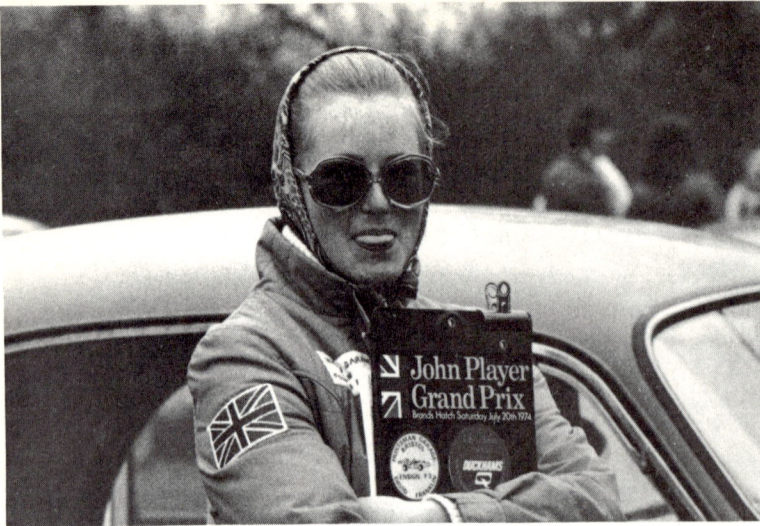

Debbie Franklin expresses pleasure at the
result of husband David's last run at
Curborough

his performances at those which he did attend, were exceptionally good. He came through to take a fine sixth
place overall in the series. David concentrated on the Guyson/BARC Hillclimb series, a difficult one for a single
seater to win, but meteoric performances, especially at the end of the year, saw him emerge as the overall
champion. Even that, however, was not the end of the successes for the almost invincible Huntsman Ensign, for
in his spare weekends, he also took in as many of the RAC Sprint Championship events as he could manage. He
often provided a thorn in the side of much more potent machinery, eventually finishing a stirring second overall
in that series. David also ventured onto the Continent with the car, and proved equally at home on the longer
European hills, taking a fine class win with a new record, at the Swiss hill of San Ursanne Les Rangiers, in the
process defeating many of the top European drivers with their modern F2 racing cars.

1976 saw David Franklin making the last step up the ladder into the large racing car class, with a March
742 powered by the BMW F2 racing engine. As one might expect, it took him a little time to sort out the new
and much more powerful car, but he really applied himself to the task in hand, and when success came, it was in
a big way. Having never visited the Channel Islands hills in the past, David, in his quest for championship points,
with the now Wendy Wools sponsored car, decided to contest both the Bouley Bay round and the Les Val Des
Terres event. He finished seventh at Bouley, a result which disappointed him a little, but two days later, after a
trip across the water from Jersey to Guernsey, the story was very different, for despite visiting the hill, which is
amongst the most difficult in the RAC series, for the first time, he was in tremendous form, taking his first ever
major win. David, also, by the end of the year had really announced his arrival, for at the penultimate round of
the championship at Prescott, he again found his top form, not only winning the event, ahead of 'The King of
Prescott', Roy Lane, but also breaking the outright record, which Roy had held for four years. David eventually
finished fourth overall in the championship, and coupled this with a fine third place, in the now annual Swiss
event, and excellent showings at all the events he contested. The slightly balding Bristolian has already
accumulated a tremendous record, and must be one of the men to really watch in the future.

Mike MacDowel

To trace Mike MacDowel's motor racing past, one has to almost delve into the archives, for the man, who is
a director of John Coombe's, the Jaguar garage at Guildford, was circuit racing almost two decades ago, with more
than a fair amount of success. Mike came into hillclimbing, not surprisingly, with a Jaguar E type, which he
shared with Bob Jennings, and then progressed into single seater racing cars showing a great deal of potential. It
was in 1973 that Mike, after several racing cars, seemed to hit on the right combination, a 5 litre Repco engined
Brabham BT36X, and with a storming performance at the latter end of the season, he emerged as the RAC
Hillclimb Champion. 1974 saw Mike again well in command at most events, and he swept almost serenely to
his second championship win, only failing by one point to secure the title with a maximum points score, a feat
hitherto unachieved. With two championship wins under his belt, Mike retired from single seater racing for a
season, and fielded a Chevron B19 sports racing car, for a season of fun, in 1975. However, the single seater bug
would not lie down, and to everyone's delight, he was back seriously contesting the championship in 1976, with
a two litre engined Ralt, the smallest single seater he had driven in the series. Mike soon started to show all his
old form with the small engined car, and despite not winning a championship round, just snatched fifth place in
the series from Sir Nicholas Williamson.

After a year away from single seaters, Mike MacDowel returned in 1976 with a Ralt RT1 powered by a Hart 420R 2 litre engine, the first appearance of the marque. He quickly showed that he had lost none of his old magic by taking the car to fifth place in the RAC Hillclimb Championship

Sir Nicholas Williamson

Sir Nicholas Williamson must be rated as the hardest trying driver in modern hillclimbing, for the sight and sound of the Reading baronet in full cry with his March 741 DFV Formula One car, has to be seen to be believed. Twice RAC Hillclimb Champion, in 1970 and 1972, he retired in 1975, but he too could not resist the temptation to return the following year. It was a fraught season for him, but, as always, he really pressed on as only he can, exciting crowds throughout Great Britain with his spectacular driving style. Ironically perhaps, his one championship win with the March during 1976, saw an almost subdued Sir Nicholas, for at Bouley Bay he was in a class of his own, the car never once sliding or twitching, as he proved in the morning practice session by shattering the existing Chris Cramer hill record. This feat he repeated exactly to within one hundredth of a second in the vital championship run-off later in the day, to put his name in the record books, and take his first, and as it materialised, his only win of the year. However, Sir Nicholas's spirited drives throughout the season finally netted him sixth place overall in the series, but we may be robbed of the sight of the enthusiastic pilot rushing up the hills next year, as Roy Lane has bought the car, and it may be that we shall only see Sir Nicholas Williamson hillclimbing his delightful Jaguar D type in the sports racing car class. There are many people, who although appreciating greatly the delights of the Jaguar, feverently hope that the baronet will again be seen at the wheel of a single seater in an effort to take his third hillclimb championship.

One of the really push-on drivers, Sir Nicholas Williamson, can always be relied upon to excite the crowds with his March 741 DFV, or in fact any car he uses

Ken MacMaster

Ken MacMaster is another man who came into the world of hillclimbing at the wheel of a saloon car, for several seasons, like David Franklin, campaigning a full race Hillman Imp. Ken also graduated into the racing car class with an Imp engined car, the very pretty Ginetta G17, and his smooth and exceptionally neat driving style, saw him well up with the pacemakers. He graduated into the 1600cc class with a GRD, the first car of this marque to appear on the hills and shocked everyone with a fine fastest time of the day at the BARC championship round at Loton Park very early in the season, a performance he followed up with very consistent performances indeed. For 1975 Ken, always a man to surprise the hillclimb world, appeared with a brand new Modus M4 powered by a Hart two litre engine, and again started to show potential. However, despite some extremely consistent drives, Ken proved unable to secure an outright win, but his extremely consistent drives were rewarded with fifth place overall in the championship.

For 1976 Ken retained the same car, and again drove with his own brand of tidiness, although the pressure at the top of the championship table was extreme. Towards the middle of the season Ken had resigned himself to another season of regular finishes, but no victories, but hillclimbing is an unpredictable game, and two weeks after David Franklins' surprise victory in Guernsey, it was Ken's turn, for whilst the hot favourites for the Pontypool event all made slight mistakes when it mattered, Ken drove in his usual unruffled manner, and was rewarded with his first, and extremely popular RAC Championship event win. Although he dropped back to seventh in the 1976 championship, Ken MacMaster was always right with the pacemakers, and must certainly be rated as one of the tidiest drivers ever seen in British hillclimbing.

The Modus M4 of Ken MacMaster, one of the tidiest drivers in modern day hillclimbing

Martyn Griffiths

Martyn Griffiths is another man who found it impossible to retire from the sport of hillclimbing. Having competed for several years in a Mallock U2 and a Lotus 41, Martyn then retired from the sport for a few seasons, but in 1974 the magnetism had worked, and he was back. He purchased a Mallock U2, and a reasonably inexpensive Ford Twin Cam engine, to, in his own words, "Tool about, and have some fun". Not even Martyn could have anticipated the success which was to come in that year, for he really became the pacemaker in the up to 1600cc sports racing car class, and by the halfway point in the season was unbeaten, and leading the RAC Leaders Hillclimb Championship. From then on he realised that from a humble beginning at the start of the season, real success was possible, and he made no mistakes, going on to take the championship, which he never even really set out to contest.

Having reverted to a 2 litre March from the 5 litre McLaren, Martyn Griffiths took the Severn Advertising car to eighth place in the 1976 RAC Hillclimb Championship

In his first year of championship hillclimbing with this Chevrolet engined McLaren M10B, Martyn Griffiths finished a creditable tenth overall in the series

The next season saw Martyn making a monumental step, from the 1600cc Mallock U2 to a 5 litre McLaren M10B Chevrolet single seater with which to contest the RAC Hillclimb Championship. He made the transition well, despite a rather nasty accident at Pontypool, and once settled in, made the large car go extremely well. By getting into the top ten run-off for championship points consistently, Martyn gradually added to his championship score, and then really secured a finishing place in the top ten overall by winning the almost boycotted Craigantlet event in Northern Ireland. For 1976 Martyn decided to go back to a smaller engined car, and purchased the Chris Cramer March 74B. As with the earlier U2, he looked happy with a smaller engine, and really set about making his mark on the championship scene, often finishing in the top half dozen at the qualifying events. He improved his previous year's championship finishing position by two places, to eighth. There can be no doubt, that in the next few seasons, the Severn Advertising cars of Martyn Griffiths will be amongst the leading competitors in the world of British speed hillclimbing.

John Cussins

John Cussins, the managing director of the well known furnishing house, Waring and Gillow, has been competing in hillclimbs for many seasons, although he also has retired for brief spells during his foray into the sport. Having returned to the sport in 1974, he shared the Waring and Gillow supported Brabham BT35X Repco with his transport director Malcolm Dungworth. However, for 1975, a new car was purchased for the team; a brand new Chevron B32 single seater racing car, powered of course by the ubiquitous Chevrolet V8 engine. Malcolm retained the Brabham, whilst John fielded the Chevron, but this proved a mighty machine from which to sort the bugs. John has always been a fiery driver, his, at times, almost frightening efforts in the Chevron

frequently kept him in the hunt for points. Ironically, however, his best 1975 result came at the wheel of a Brabham. At the Barbon Manor meeting, a drive shaft broke on the Chevron, causing a considerable amount of damage to the rear suspension; with this certainly not repairable in the lunch interval between practice and the event. John took over the wheel of the Brabham, the car with which he had won the Barbon event in 1974. Suitably annoyed at the problems with the Chevron, John was in a devastating mood and really threw the Brabham to the top of the hill in tremendous style, to win the event. 1976 saw John really struggling with the Chevron, which never seemed to quite produce the potential, and with the opposition even stronger, John was relegated to ninth place in the championship at the end of the year, a position he is obviously capable of improving on in the future.

A nice action shot of Rob Turnbull, the sensation of the 1600cc racing car class in 1976, on his way to a class win at Bouley Bay. This was his first appearance on the hill where he immediately made his mark by breaking the class record

Rob Turnbull

Rob Turnbull, a transport company director from Sutton Coldfield, really arrived on the hillclimb scene in 1976 with a big bang. Originally, Rob started his motor sporting career in the world of sprinting with an Alexis, taking in during the season, a Shelsley Walsh hillclimb. The real turning point, for the then slightly wild driver, came upon the purchasing of a Brabham BT35 fitted with a Ford BDA engine. He really started to motor well, especially on the twistier sprint courses, often giving the V8 powered cars something to think about. Realising that the Brabham was ideally suited to the twistier venues, Rob started to take in more hillclimbs at the expense of sprints and proved himself to be developing into an extremely rapid driver indeed, having lost his original raggedness, becoming a very smooth pilot indeed.

1975 brought a considerable amount of success for the B & W Motors sponsored car, but 1976 was really his year. In over 30 events, he suffered defeat just three times in the class, at times posting results that would be excellent for a two litre car, let alone a 1600cc powered one. Throughout the year, he proved more than capable of challenging even the top pacemakers in hillclimbing, qualifying for many top ten run-offs and becoming the first man ever to climb Shelsley Walsh in under 30 seconds with a 1600cc engined car. Rob, however, had set his sights on finishing in the top ten of the RAC Hillclimb Championship, a massive target, but one which he looked like achieving. However, the pace was furious, and some excellent performances by Surtees driver Richard Jones, suddenly looked like robbing the Sutton Coldfield driver of his tenth place. It all rested on the final round at Doune, where Rob rose to the occasion magnificently, climbing the Scottish hill over two seconds faster than any 1600cc car in the past, and no-one could deny him his tenth place in the series. He gave everything in his efforts to achieve that position which many would have said was well beyond reach. For 1977 Rob, like Mike MacDowel will be fielding a two litre Ralt, and really must be in with a very good chance indeed of posing the current championship pacemakers a real problem.

Dave Harris

Dave Harris must rate as one of the true all rounders in motor sport, for having started his career with a Ford Cortina taking part in a special stage rally in Wales, he has also tried his hand at most other forms of four wheeled competition with the exception of circuit racing. Like David Franklin, he really started to make his name on the autocross scene, firstly at the wheel of a Riley 1.5, and later with an MGB. David, right from the word go, began amassing awards during the summer autocross season, also occasionally taking in a sprint or hillclimb with the same car, whilst he amused himself during the winter with a spot of production car trailing. His first real effort in a single seater racing car was at the Weston Speed Trials, behind the wheel of Geoff Inglis' supercharged Brabham, and his appetite for tarmac events was whetted. It was, in fact, the ex Inglis March 702 which gave Dave his first real season of sprinting and he soon came to grips with the sport, starting to make an impression immediately. However, it was 1974 which saw him coming to the fore in sprinting, when he acquired the McLaren M10B Chevrolet which was to see him through the next three seasons.

1974 was a good start with the V8 engined car, with Dave taking second place overall in the RAC Sprint Championship. He retained the car for 1975, and really dominated the series, especially at the faster venues, easily taking the title which had just eluded him the previous year. However, the story was a little different in 1976, for although he started the season well, the opposition was much fiercer and he found it more difficult to open a large lead in the championship. Just beyond the half way point in the season, his chances of retaining the championship looked slim, as he blew up the McLaren engine. With Harris already under considerable pressure from the pursuing Formula 1 Lotus of David Render and the Brabham BT33 of Simon Riley, the cause looked lost. It was fellow Bristolian Terry Smith, who came to the champion's rescue, by sharing his McLaren M14D with Harris. Harris rapidly adapted himself to the new mount and kept the pressure on, finally just clinching the title for the second year. After three seasons with the McLaren which had taken him to two championships and a second place, Dave has now replaced the car with the ex Roy Lane McRae, and must surely be in with a very good chance of completing the hat trick of sprint championship wins. Certainly the car is tremendous, as Roy himself proved at the end of 1976, taking the car to the Weston Speed Trials, where not only did he wipe the board even with the experienced sprinters, but broke the outright record, on his one and only practice run. He repeated the performance all the way through the meeting, finally reducing it to an almost unbelievable mark. Even Dave Harris in the same car could well find it hard to beat the time set by Lane during his last ever drive in the car.

Possibly the fastest McLaren M10B Chevrolet in recent years, this car has taken Bristol garage owner Dave Harris to two consecutive sprint championship titles

David Render

David Render, a quarry owner from London, openly admits to being 'not as young as some', but age brings experience, and there can be no more qualified sprinter than Render. David has been both hillclimbing and sprinting for many seasons with a variety of cars from Minis, to a V8 engined Ginetta sports racing car, and his latest acquisition, the ex works Lotus 76 Formula One Grand Prix car. David obtained the Lotus with the 1976 season a quarter completed, but already by that time he was well placed in the sprint championship, after some excellent drives in his two litre Brabham BT35. Almost against expectations he rapidly accustomed himself to the incredible Lotus and really started to fly, especially on the fastest sprint courses. He began, as the season progressed, to close the gap on the championship leader Harris, and at one time looked like catching him. However, despite some great drives, which included an incredible course record at Bassingbourn, averaging well over 100mph from the standing start for the 1600 yard course, and a fine win in the championship run-off at Weston, Render was to be denied the championship he has fought so hard to win over the past years. However, David was slightly consoled during the season, as he achieved his other ambition, an outright win in the historic Brighton Speed Trials. Although the runner up in 1976, he will still battle on for the championship, and could well still achieve that ambition. David Render is highly respected as a driver, and 'the ambassador of British sprinting,' for in the history of the sport, no one competitor has worked so hard, both on and off the track, to make sprinting the success that it has become.

Although mainly a sprint exponent, David Render has also been seen trying his hand at hillclimbs, with amongst other cars, this 1600cc BDA engined Brabham BT29X

Simon Riley

Like many competitors in sprinting and hillclimbing today, Simon Riley began his active participation of the sport, on the other side of the fence, as a marshal. He began his competitive career at Wiscombe Park, sharing his father's Jaguar saloon at the Aston Martin Owners Club event, but it was soon realised that the Jaguar was a rather cumbersome car for such events, and a Lotus 7 appeared. The car was run for several seasons, finally being fitted with a turbocharger, and success came with several class wins, as well as dramas. Simon was unlucky to invert the car at the Bodiam Hillclimb, fortunately without serious damage. Although Simon still owns the Lotus, it was time to graduate to single seater racing cars, and he acquired a Brabham BT30. However, success on the hills was hard to come by in the competitive up to 1600cc racing car class, and it was decided to try the sprint scene.

For 1975, Simon chose the very popular McLaren M10B, fitted not with the customary Chevrolet engine, but a Rover version. Although the car occasionally proved competitive, Simon was plagued with engine problems, which really ruined what could have been a reasonable season. However, 1975, was the year that saw the sprint scene erupting with competitive cars, and so for the following year, Simon acquired the Tony Griffiths Brabham

Although basically a sprinter, Simon Riley with the distinctive Monsieur Houbigant Brabham BT33 DFV, also ventured onto the hills

BT33 DFV Formula One car. As in the previous year, Simon was sponsored by the Monsieur Houbigant perfume house, and the car repainted in the familiar draughtboard livery. Once accustomed to the car, Simon began to fly, and developed from a mid-field runner into a pacemaker, setting the fastest time of the day at the Blackpool round and winning the championship run-off at the first Bassingbourn event, in the process setting, what was to prove at the latter, a short lived course record. Throughout the year Simon remained competitive, and always looked to be in the championship hunt, finally finishing third, a position which this young London driver could well better in forthcoming seasons.

Johnty Williamson

Like David Render, Johnty Williamson has been involved with the sport of sprinting for many seasons, often also taking in a few hillclimbs. It was in fact Johnty, way back in 1971, who won the second ever RAC Sprint Championship, and since then he has always been amongst the pacemakers. For the last two years, Johnty has campaigned the Formula 5000 Surtees TS11 Chevrolet, under the banners of the Manpower Employment Agency, and Uni-Rents Tools. In 1976 he still proved that he is capable of challenging the newcomers into the sport, with a consistent series of performances which took him to fourth place overall in the sprint championship. A real character, in more senses than one, Johnty can be relied upon to enliven the proceedings at any event with his own dry humour, which in fact typifies the total fun loving attitude of the majority of sprinters and hillclimbers in Great Britain today.

Bob Rose

Midlander Bob Rose, like his near neighbour Rob Turnbull, is in the transport business and certainly knows all about high speed travel, having successfully competed in hillclimbs, sprints and circuit races during his long career. Having retired from circuit racing, Bob took to sprinting single seater racing cars, and his name is now synonymous with the Curborough Sprint venue, for he has won more events there than anyone. However, Bob has proved extremely competitive at all the venues in the sprint championship, having taken the title in 1972 with a McLaren M10B, and in 1974 with the M14D model. Bob Rose is a wiley competitor, who is very difficult to beat, and although not prominent on the sprint scene in 1976, having sold his car, could well be back to attempt to take his hat trick of Sprint Championships, and reclaim the Curborough record from the Token Formula One car of John Ravenscroft, who deposed Rose as 'The King of Curborough' in 1976.

Russ Ward

Our quick look at some of the competitors would not be complete without a few of the drivers of non-racing cars. One such man is Russ Ward, an electrical engineer from Churchdown near Cheltenham, who has two natural abilities. The first is to drive his supercharged Austin Healey Sprite incredibly rapidly, and the second is a natural talent for clowning. Firstly, let us look at Russ' competition career, and it really is a success story. Having acquired an Austin Healey Sprite in the mid 1960s, Russ took to the autocross fields, and really threw the car around with gay abandon, often coming away with a major award, always being right in the hunt at the end of the day. With the interest in autocrossing beginning to dwindle, Russ decided to take to hillclimbs with the same car. Almost immediately he made his impression, and in 1974 made his mark in the Leaders Hillclimb Championship, and already was marked down as a man to watch. For 1975, he appeared with the car supercharged, and

Russ 'Puff' Ward, the genial winner of the RAC Leaders Hillclimb Championship in 1976 with his supercharged John Brown Motors Austin Healey Sprite

looked like a likely candidate for victory, but he was plagued with minor maladies, and finally was forced to concede defeat to the supercharged Gryphon of Cheltenham compatriate Alan Richards.

However, 1976 was Russ Ward's year, for the howling Sprite, which for several seasons had appeared in the livery of John Brown Motors, rewarded the sponsor with an almost unblemished record, conceding defeat just once, and going on after three seasons of effort to take the long sought after championship. It was not an easy win for Russ however, for despite some incredible record breaking runs, including the first sub 50 second climb of Prescott in a sports car, he was chased every inch of the way by the Brabham of Chris Dowson, who eventually lost the Leaders Championship to Ward on the tie-break rule, having also, like Ward, scored maximum points in the series. Russ Ward's championship win, however, was most popular, for this tall fun loving engineer from Churchdown brings to the paddock more than a little light relief. Not only does he thoroughly enjoy his competitive sport, but also the natural atmosphere of fun. Russ Ward is one of hillclimbing's real characters, and hopefully will remain on the hills for many years to come.

Chris Dowson

Chris Dowson has been competing in hillclimbs for several years, especially in the historic class, but in 1976 the Pershore farmer decided to contest seriously the Leaders Hillclimb Championship. It was the first time that Chris had visited some of the championship hills during 1976, but he really dominated the up to 1100cc racing car class with his supercharged Brabham. He really proved to be a thorn in the side of Russ Ward in the Leaders Hillclimb Championship, and very nearly clinched the championship, failing only due to a broken drive shaft, which sidelined him at a Shelsley meeting. For a first serious attempt at the championship it was an impressive effort, and with a new engine planned for 1977, it could be his year.

In his first year of championship hillclimbing, Chris Dowson with his supercharged Brabham BT15 Ford only failed by a whisker to take victory in the RAC Leaders Hillclimb Championship

Barry Brant

Some 25 years after its inception, the Cooper 500 racing car lives on. One of the real stalwarts of the historic racing car brigade is central heating engineer Barry Brant from Birmingham. Barry, with his Triumph motorcycle engined Cooper MkX, has been competing in hillclimbs for many seasons, always with success. Despite being a little on the tall side, Barry wedges his length into the diminutive little car, and his driving style, which to put it mildly is enthusiastic, has earned him the nickname of 'Elbows'. Despite the fact that his car is now advancing in years, he still proves capable of challenging the quicker of the modern cars in the up to 500cc racing car class and, in fact, finished a remarkable third overall in the 1975 RAC Leaders Hillclimb Championship. So as you can see, the Cooper is still alive and well, thanks to the dedicated efforts of a bunch of enthusiasts such as Barry, and with the interest in such cars being rapidly revitalised, Barry and his fellow competitors should still be seen for many years to come.

Barry Brant demonstrates how he acquired the nickname of 'Elbows' as he flings his Cooper Mk X Triumph through The Ashes at Gurston Down

John Meredith

One of the stalwarts of the saloon car class, John Meredith and his Mini Cooper S have become a natural part of any hillclimb season. To list the successes of the Leighton Buzzard driver would take far too much space, but suffice to say that he has been rarely beaten, and has set the pace in the class in the last few years. Saloon car hillclimbing is very competitive indeed, but John has generally managed to keep the upper hand at most meetings, and has always excelled in the championships which he has entered. 1976 was a particularly good year for the balding Mini driver, for he led the Guyson/BARC Hillclimb Championship for much of the year, before finally losing to Charles Barter, whilst his ability to fight back after dramas was also ably demonstrated. The final Wiscombe Park hillclimb of the year, which was also a round of the Guyson/BARC hillclimb series, saw John fighting hard to maintain his lead at the head of the championship table with the Mini. On his first run disaster struck, for he lost control at the top of the Esses, and plunged into the undergrowth, slightly damaging the car. However, the Mini was retrieved during the lunch break, and undaunted, John re-appeared in the afternoon, finally setting a personal best time for Wiscombe, a fine recovery indeed. It may well be that the mistake at Wiscombe cost John the Guyson/BARC Hillclimb Championship for 1976, but the fighting spirit which he showed at Wiscombe will almost certainly prevail, and there is a strong possibility that the man who climbed Prescott in a saloon car for the first time ever in under 50 seconds, could well take a major National hillclimb championship before long.

Stuart Watts

There are many exceptionally successful competitors from Wales, all of whom bring the sport their own infectious humour. One such man is Haverfordwest dentist Stuart Watts, who for the past few seasons has been concentrating on the Guyson/BARC Hillclimb Championship with his extremely fleet Lotus Elan. Despite the fact that he often has many hundreds of miles to travel to an event, Stuart has always been at the top of the sports car class. His success rate has been phenomenal, with the combination now holding many class records at the major venues in Great Britain. Stuart really has given his all in an attempt to win the Guyson/BARC Hillclimb Championship, and very nearly achieved this aim in 1975. He needed a good performance in the last event of the year, at Harewood in Yorkshire, to deprive David Franklin of the title, and being in top form as he started the event, he certainly proved a major threat. However, unfortunately for Stuart, after the long trek from West Wales, the weather at the Harewood event turned sour, and with the course slippery, he was unable, despite his excellent form, to quite post the time necessary to take the title. However, with a new car on the stocks, he will certainly be a man to beat in the class in 1977. Like several other competitors, Stuart is also actively involved with his local motor club, and along with the Morris brothers, is the driving force behind the excellent Talbenny Sprint, a meeting which typifies the approach of the Welsh in motor sport, being extremely well run, and above all retaining a free and easy atmosphere.

There are of course throughout the country, many other drivers worthy of a mention, such people as Charles Barter, the pipe smoking driver of the Golden Springs Watercress Hillman Imp, who in his first season of really competitive hillclimbing won the Guyson/BARC Hillclimb Championship outright. Bristol McLaren driver Terry Smith, a sprint championship round winner in 1976, Peter Kaye, the bearded Brabham driver from Yorkshire, who after a successful apprenticeship in Minis has really graduated to single seater racing cars in a big way, and Jeremy Lord, the former circuit racing champion who returned to hillclimbs in 1976, and carried on breaking records where he had left off a few years earlier. There are also many drivers who are totally dedicated to the sport, supporting meetings at every opportunity, and yet in many cases never savouring victory. The latter are, of course, the backbone of the sport, but win or lose, every competitor without exception is vital to the sport, for without them, where would we be? Ladies and gentlemen we thank you.

Press and publicity

Having got this far, and we hope found that you are interested in the sport of hillclimbing and sprinting, the next stage will be to see an event in the flesh, but how do you find out where and when the events are taking place. Well there are several ways.

The first, and probably the best guide to what is happening within the sport, is to follow the motor sporting press, who are fully informed as to all events, championships and any other interesting points which might occur. There are two regular magazines in Great Britain which cover all aspects of sprinting and hillclimbing, and both are published weekly. There is the newspaper format *Motoring News,* whilst taking the form of a glossy colour front page magazine is *Autosport.* Both give good coverage to the forthcoming events, whilst also reporting in detail on the previous week's events, and they are a very good guide indeed as to what is taking place within the sport.

If there is an event in your own particular area, then there is a fair chance that the local newspapers and television companies will cover it in detail. They will usually give a very good preview of the type of event you can expect as well as listing the star names who will be competing. In the last few years local radio stations have sprung up throughout the country, and many take more than an active interest in the local events, the fortunes of local drivers, even outside their normal coverage area. One such local channel is Radio Bristol, who not only invariably provide excellent pre-event information, but also feature live reports of some of the events in their sports programme, and have also carried reports of meetings from well outside their own area when local drivers have been involved.

The organisers of any event, as you will have seen earlier, will be keen to publicise their meeting, and a watchful eye at local level will invariably inform you of an event in the area.

Ode to a hill climber

He came to the line with gentle care,
Blipping the throttle, the power's still there,
The light turned green, the driver saw red,
With wheelspin and snaking, off the line he sped.
The first part was steep, so he piled on the power,
The track still damp, he cursed that shower.

Up to the first bend, this is the one,
When if taken flat-out provides the fun,
But he's a tough one, it's flat out all the way.
Never mind if the tail turns the grass bank to hay,
With engine screaming he wended his way,
To the top of the hill, it must be fastest today.

He came to the Esses doing ninety miles an hour,
The front wheels locked, he took off the power,
He flicked it left, the tail went right,
Oh isn't this man a thrilling sight.
With flick of wrists, and burst of power,
It straightens up, it might beat the hour!

But even then, there's still one more bend,
Before he sights this hillclimb's end,
The top Esses bend approached so fast,
Oh could he get it right at last?
What was it that the champion said,
He aimed for the drain as the power he fed.

He's trailing the field, so he gave it a try,
He clipped that drain, and the revs rose sky high,
But still he kept that right foot down,
He could rob the champion of that crown.
He was trying hard, and it showed so clear,
As his elbows waved, no sign of fear.

At last he saw the straight for home,
So he crouched right down, at the mouth there was foam,
With man and car twitching as one,
At speed he reckoned this was fun.
As over the line he flashed so fast,
His time, oh no, again he was last.

Appendix 1
Motorcycles

Over the past few years, the motorcycle following in both hillclimbs and sprints has increased dramatically, and both the solo machines and the combinations can make a particularly exciting spectacle, as they, just like the cars, fight their way to the finish at exceptionally high speeds. The margin for error, especially with a solo motorcycle, is even smaller than with a car, for with just two narrow tyres to hold the machine on the road, the slightest mistake can mean a nasty tumble, and often injury. This fails to deter the two wheeled rider, whose enthusiasm matches that of the regular car competitor.

The standard ware for solo motorcycle hillclimbing are basically not the most modern of racing machines, although over the last few years some very rapid machinery has begun to find its way onto the courses. They have proved exceptionally fast, often managing to climb a course faster than some of the smaller engined racing cars. Basically, it is a small select band who regularly compete in hillclimbs, and this allows the motorcycles to appear at the same meetings as the cars, thus providing additional spectator interest. The National Sprint Association are extremely active in Great Britain, and now also stage all motorcycle meetings at such venues as Barbon Manor and Wiscombe Park, as well as running a National Motorcycle Speed Hillclimb Championship. The championship really has become the domain of Paul Spargo with his Ariel/Triumph. He has totally dominated the series in the last few years. Although he must be one of the tallest regular motorcycle racers, Paul manages to curl around his machine, and his progress is truly tremendous as he fights his powerful bike through the bends on a hillclimb. Such has been his prowess in the past few seasons that he is normally never challenged for victory by his motorcycle compatriots, and there are very few outright hill records that this expatriated Cornishman does not hold.

However, despite Paul's superiority, the motorcycle classes always provide excellent spectator entertainment, with the 250cc machines never ceasing to amaze as they regularly defeat the larger engined bikes. People like Dave Brierly with his Zunspec, provide good entertainment, with another Cornishman, Neville Tregembo, always in contention with his TPR Yamaha, whilst of the up to 500cc machines, it is usually the Velocette of many times 500cc champion Peter Isaac who leads the way. He often comes under considerable pressure from the easily recognised Arnold Gimblett, who invariably completes his climbs on his Triumph/Norton clad in his familiar red sweater which has earned him the name of 'The Red Devil'.

Naturally it is the Ariel/Triumph of Paul Spargo which leads the way in the largest of the motorcycle classes, whilst amongst the favourites in the sidecar division are the very fleet combination of Dave Skinner and passenger Tim Johnson with their class record holding Greenwood, which proved so controversial when first announced a few years ago for circuit racing.

Although not every car hillclimb contains a class for motorcycles, they are becoming increasingly popular with both organisers, and spectators alike, and they will continue to flourish as long as these brave men are prepared to compete. That looks like a long time yet, and with general motorcycle interest rapidly developing, it will bring an influx of new and even more exciting machines, onto the hillclimb and sprint courses of the country.

Sidecar hillclimbing is only for the brave. Here the passenger is within an ace of contacting a solid object as he leans out to stabilise the outfit

Motorcycle hillclimbing can be wearing on the soles of the feet

Like their car counterparts, the motorcycle hillclimbers and sprinters also use road going machines

Three motorcycle sprinters awaiting their turn

Appendix 2 The RAC: their part in the sport

Like any active sport, hillclimbing and sprinting is operated within a rigid framework of rules and regulations, and answerable to a governing body. In this instance it is the Motor Sport Division of the Royal Automobile Club. This organisation governs virtually the whole of the organised British motor sport and is, as you would expect, a thoroughly professional organisation.

The rules and regulations for hillclimbing and sprinting are formulated by the RAC with help from various competitors who will sit on the special Speed Competitions Committee. They assist with the day to day running of the RAC, in that all problems and queries are discussed at these meetings and a recommendation is passed to the general committee of the RAC, who may implement or reject the recommendation as they see fit. The speed committee however is a fairly recent innovation, and provides the competitors themselves with a direct opportunity of representation at the RAC. Although still in its infancy, it is proving an invaluable asset in liason between the average competitor and the actual governing body, who finally set their seal on, and implement, new rules and regulations.

The RAC themselves are also responsible for the National Hillclimb Championship, and the Leaders Hillclimb series, and although they do not directly organise the qualifying rounds, leaving this to individual clubs, they select the various qualifying rounds and actually formulate the championship positions from the results supplied by the organising clubs. In addition to the two hillclimb championships, the RAC also govern the National Sprint Championship which is sponsored by the Haynes Publishing Group.

It is the RAC who sanction each hillclimb or sprint event, and inspect and issue track licences to allow a venue to be used. Once a meeting is sanctioned, and the permit to run the contest issued, the RAC will also nominate an official representative to attend the meeting as a steward to report back to headquarters on the general conduct of the event. In addition to issuing track and meeting permits, a budding competitor must obtain from the RAC a competitions licence before taking part in an event, whilst all the clubs who organise major motor sport will also be registered with the Motor Sport Division.

To list all the functions of the RAC would again take up much too much space, but suffice to say that they are the governors of British hillclimbing and sprinting. Like most governors, they are often criticised, but generally they do an excellent job in making sure that all forms of British motor sport are properly organised, thus ensuring a high standard throughout the country.

Appendix 3 World record attempts

Whilst there are very few people in this country who have not at some time or another been attracted by the outright land speed record, and the publicity that goes with each attempt, there are on the other hand, very few people that realise there are many more World speed records which can be attempted, many with a normal hillclimb or sprint car.

Before looking at the World record attempts themselves, let us take a look at the National records scene, and it really is a substantial area of the sport of sprinting. As in a conventional sprint there are many classes, in fact more than will be generally found at a normal sprint event, and cars of all types and capacities are catered for, ranging from the up to 250cc machines, basically supported by the faster go-karts in the country, to the massive over eight litre car class which allows such machines as outright dragsters to vie for National, and even International records. Within each class there are no less than eight records to aim for, a quarter of a mile run, a half kilometer and a full kilometer run, as well as a full mile, and there are records for both standing start runs and flying start runs. Any driver can attempt a record breaking run at any time with authorisation from the RAC, who again govern the record breaking attempts, but the onus is on the competitor to arrange his own venue, officials and timekeepers and this can be an expensive process. However, the airfield at Elvington has become the home of British record attempts and, as such, stages organised record attempts. The most popular meeting is organised in early October, and this enables all the would-be record breakers to make their attempts over the chosen length course at the weekend, thus reducing the financial outlay considerably.

Although there are also World records for each of the classes which are run for the National record breaking attempts, they are by no means out of reach of many of the club sprint and hillclimb drivers, and no less than twenty eight such records are at present held by British Nationals. However, many of the existing National and World records are now rather outdated, with some of the National records stretching back to as long ago as 1923, whilst of the World records, there are many which have now been standing for nearly ten years, and must shortly be beaten. As we have said sprint and hillclimb cars are more than capable of putting their names in the record books. This has been well proved in the past, particularly by Miss Patsy Burt, who with her hillclimb McLaren single seater racing car, holds no less than nine National records, and three World records. Even the saloon cars can figure well in the smaller capacity classes as Mini driver Ed Spencer proved, taking the National class record for the flying half kilometer course with his 1300cc Mini Cooper S.

The main requirement for record breaking is a reasonably rapid car for the appropriate class, and a reliable one, for the record attempt stipulates that a run must be made in each direction over the course, and the record is based on the average time and speed for the two runs. Record breaking has not seen a tremendous upsurge in interest in the last few years but with many records now ageing rapidly, it will not be long before new interest is shown, and many new names are added to both the National and International records lists in the many classes.

Appendix 4
Championship winners through the years

RAC Hillclimb Championship

1947	Raymond Mays
1948	Raymond Mays
1949	Sydney Allard
1950	Dennis Poore
1951	Ken Wharton
1952	Ken Wharton
1953	Ken Wharton
1954	Ken Wharton
1955	Tony Marsh
1956	Tony Marsh
1957	Tony Marsh
1958	David Boshier-Jones
1959	David Boshier-Jones
1960	David Boshier-Jones
1961	David Good
1962	Arthur Owen
1963	Peter Westbury
1964	Peter Westbury
1965	Tony Marsh
1966	Tony Marsh
1967	Tony Marsh
1968	Peter Lawson
1969	David Hepworth
1970	Sir Nicholas Williamson
1971	David Hepworth
1972	Sir Nicholas Williamson
1973	Mike MacDowel
1974	Mike MacDowel
1975	Roy Lane
1976	Roy Lane

RAC Leaders Hillclimb Championship

1970	Chris Cramer
1971	Tony Bancroft
1972	Chris Cramer
1973	Alex Brown
1974	Martyn Griffiths
1975	Alan Richards
1976	Russ Ward

BARC Hillclimb Championship

1968	Jeff Goodliffe
1969	Jeff Goodliffe
1970	Jeff Goodliffe
1971	Jim Thomson
1972	Chris Seaman
1973	Mike Flather
1974	Peter Voigt
1975	David Franklin
1976	Charles Barter

RAC Sprint Championship

1970	Miss Patsy Burt
1971	Johnty Williamson
1972	Bob Rose
1973	John Ravenscroft
1974	Bob Rose
1975	David Harris
1976	David Harris

A galley of photographs

It could be argued that hillclimbing and sprinting sees a much wider cross section of cars than another form of motor sport. To enforce this theory we are showing a number of photographs of a wide variety of the cars which have appeared over the past two years of competition.

The single seater cars are often hard to tell apart whereas the saloon and GT cars are always obvious. A full caption is given with each photograph. The single seater cars are shown first, followed by the saloons and then the GT cars.

Bristol bodyshop proprietor Terry Smith made a big impression on the sprint scene having graduated to this 5.7 litre Chevrolet powered McLaren M14D from a 1600cc March

Typical of many of the single seater cars which compete in both hillclimbs and sprints is the Ford Twin Cam engined Brabham BT21B of Basil Thomas. He is another man to graduate to single seater cars having served his apprenticeship in a Mini

Another home built and extremely successful car is this sports racing model, the Dextra Ford, designed and built by test pilot, Dinty Moores. That the car was competitive was proved beyond all doubt by former circuit racing champion Jeremy Lord, who broke the up to 1300cc sports racing car record at Wiscombe Park in 1976

Originally built for Formula One Grand Prix racing the Token found its way onto the sprint scene in 1976 in the hands of former sprint champion John Ravenscroft, and by the end of the year had claimed the Curborough course record

The Vixen VB5 powered by the Imp engine and now successfully driven by Chris Bigwood, is possibly one of the most successful small engined single seater racing cars of all time, having taken both David Franklin and Terry Smith to ennumerable wins before they graduated into the largest of the racing car classes

Simon Phillips proves equally at home whether it be long distance sports car racing on the Continent or hurtling his Cooper Bristol through the long sweeping Orchard Corner at Prescott

A massive motor car for the tight confines of a hillclimb. Jerseyman Bob De La Haye fighting his Chevrolet powered Lola T142 at Bouley Bay

The Terrapin, designed by *Daily Mirror* reporter Allan Staniforth has proved a most popular car in the up to 1100cc racing car class. John Frampton, pictured, has taken many awards with his Richard Longman BMC powered version

It is encouraging to see the Formula 3 cars from immediate post war racing still alive and competing in hillclimbs. They record very creditable times

A rare sight on the hills, the Brabham BT37 DFV Formula One car campaigned by Shropshire farmer Geoff Rollason, seen here at Shelsley Walsh before selling the car to Richard Cummings for sprinting

In the past some of the faster karts have appeared in hillclimbs, despite their comparatively small 250cc motorcycle engines, proving on several occasions capable of directly competing with the faster up to 1100cc racing cars

The Lotus 31 shared in sprinting and hillclimbing by Andy Fraser and Tim Painter, despite being relatively inexpensive, has proved quite competitive, providing the two drivers with a fine grounding in single seater racing

113

Martin Steele with his Lyncar which has proved to be a car worth watching especially in sprints

Richard Jones with his very rapid 2 litre Surtees TS10 leaving the line at Doune

Roger Willoughby concentrates hard as he ushers his 3.5 litre Techcraft Buick through the Ashes Bend at Gurston Down

One of the pacemakers in the 1960s in hillclimbs, the Cooper single seater powered by a 2½ litre Daimler engine still provides a tremendous amount of fun for its current drivers

Despite running with a relatively low powered Ford BDA rally engine, this March 702 of Allan 'Bluebell' Humphries has proved to be very rapid and even captured a fastest time of the day at Wiscombe Park, proving that power alone is not the ultimate answer

Still going strong and posting some remarkable times, the Elva Formula Junior of Adrian Moores provides the enthusiastic driver with a great deal of fun at minimal expense

One of the many single seaters to use the 1600cc Formula Two FVA engine, the Ensign of electrical engineer David Way

Although rarely seen in hillclimbs and sprints, the Harrison KH4 Formula 4 car powered by the Imp engine could well be a car to watch in the up to 1100cc racing car class. Former Mini Cooper S driver Peter Shepherd, seen in action at Bouley Bay, has already shown that the car could well become a threat to the rest of the class

Still in its original trim the Lotus 35 powered by the one litre Ford MAE engine remains competitive, with driver Ken Ayers often well in the hunt for awards

Although not one of the most modern single seaters in hillclimbing, the Holbay powered Chevron B17 of Guernseyman Phil Sandwith has proved capable of scoring national championship points

Ted Dzierzek working overtime at the wheel of his Formula Atlantic Hawke during a climb of Doune

The March 733 has proved a very fine car in the up to 1600cc racing car class, and, in fact, has taken outright wins in sprinting as well as class wins on the hills

'Hang on Sloopy'

"Peek a Boo". Alister Douglas Osborn well off line at Les Val Des Terres

A big motor car for hillclimbing is the ex Formula 5000 Surtees TS8 Chevrolet seen in the hands of Stephen Cuff, the son of Wally, a prolific winner in the West Country with a Cooper JAP in the 1960s

The cars originally built for Formula Junior and Formula 3 circuit racing in the 1960s still appear on the hills today, and many like this Cooper of Roy Tostevin still lead the way in the class

A really big handful of motor car. The supercharged 3 litre Ford Capri of Wayne Wainwright. Wayne also turned to circuit racing and won the Ford Escort challenge

Graham Masters' Ford Twin Cam powered Anglia showing a distinct aversion to Sawbench Hairpin at Wiscombe Park

Always a competitive car in the saloon car class the Ford Escorts, like the Minis, come with a variety of engine sizes, the most popular being around the 1600cc mark. The car pictured has been driven by various drivers in the past, all of whom have managed to keep the L. R. Bence sponsored machine at the head of its class

A race prepared Hillman Imp, such as this one, can always be relied upon to make the Mini Cooper S work for an award in the saloon car class

You can still drive your road car to the meeting on the road, compete successfully, and then drive it home, a point more than proved by this man, Bill Holt with his Morgan +8

Although only a handful of Clan Crusaders have appeared in sprinting and hillclimbing, those which have been seen have made their mark

John Symons, a successful rallycross exponent a few seasons ago, returned to the hills with his Symonspeed prepared Mini Cooper S proving as fast on tarmac as on grass

It is all too easy to let the car take control during a sprint, the driver of this Porsche battling to keep it on the island at Yeovilton

A sight to really bring back memories. The Austin Healey 3000 which, although now a collectors item, can happily still be seen in active competition on the hills

Although at present there are no race prepared Datsun 240Zs competing in hillclimbs and sprints, there are several road going versions and they have proved to be a more than potential winner in the modified sports car classes, when tuned

The Lotus Elan proves to be one of the most competitive cars in the up to 1600cc modified sports car class

A car not often seen in hillclimbs, the Alfa Romeo of Viscount George Villiers

A rare bird and a real handful, the Allard of Fred Damodaren, a most active Scottish competitor, negotiates the twists and turns and the bottom of the Doune hillclimb

Although his every day transport, Arthur Lamy's Lotus 7, when fitted with wider wheels and suitable tyres, has proved capable of climbing his home hillclimb at Bouley Bay extremely rapidly

The supercharged CTG of former Terrapin driver Terry Duke has proved to be a very competitive car in the up to 1300cc sports racing car class

A real handful on a hill, the Corvette V8 engined Lister of John Harper, often seen competing in the popular historic sports car class

The pressure during an event is intense and even top class drivers such as Richard Brown can be caught out on occasions

"I don't think I like the rest of the hill, I think I'll go back". Gerry Ratcliffe spins at the infamous Pool Bend, Pontypool

Now you know why the photographers stand behind trees. Morgan exponent, Ray Meredith, attacks the bank at Prescott

"I don't think this line is going to work"

"Hmm, thought so"

However help is soon on hand and the damage in this case, minimal

Postscript

Well here we are, heading for the finish line. I certainly hope that you have enjoyed this book, and that you, like so many people, have found the sport of speed hillclimbing and sprinting so completely entertaining that you will join us at a meeting. If you think that this unique story may be for you, then come along and have a look, join a local motor club and maybe even marshal. I am sure that once you have seen a few events, you will be drawn into the sport, and may well want to compete. However if you do, do not rush into things, plan your approach. It can be expensive as we have seen, but if properly planned you can gain a great deal of pleasure, often for far less money than you ever imagined. If you feel that you cannot compete, then you can still savour the atmosphere of an all action meeting, either as an official, or even from behind the spectator ropes. It is a fickle sport with more than its share of ups and downs, but somehow it is never anything other than totally worthwhile, a fact that can be proved by attending a meeting and seeing a tremendous number of people indulging in the same activity, enjoying themselves. If you are already a competitor, you will know what I mean, and on my own part, I would like to take this opportunity of thanking each and every one of you, for I know that without you there would be many thousands of people whose lives would be that bit poorer. *Vive le sport!*